Property Of
Michigan Public Service Commission

RECEIVED
MICHIGAN PUBLIC SERVICE COMM.
SEP 3 1974
CHIEF OF STAFF

OFFICE OF SPECIAL STUDIES

# Regulation in Further Perspective:
# The Little Engine that Might

# Regulation in Further Perspective:

## The Little Engine that Might

Edited by
**William G. Shepherd**
**Thomas G. Gies**
*University of Michigan*

**Ballinger Publishing Company • Cambridge, Mass.**
*A Subsidiary of J.B. Lippincott Company*

Copyright © 1974 by Ballinger Publishing Company. All rights reserved. No part of this publication may be reproduced, stored in a retrieval system, or transmitted in any form or by any means, electronic, mechanical, photocopy, recording or otherwise, without the prior written consent of the publisher.

Library of Congress Catalog Card Number: 73-21991

International Standard Book Number: 0-88410-258-0

Printed in the United States of America

Library of Congress Cataloging in Publication Data
Main entry under title:
Regulation in further perspective.
   Consists chiefly of papers presented at a conference sponsored by the Interuniversity Committee on Public Utility Economics.
   Includes bibliographical references.
   1. Public utilities—United States—Rate of return—Congresses. 2. Public utilities—United States—Rates—Congresses. I. Shepherd, William G., ed. II. Gies, Thomas George, 1921–    ed. III. Inter-university Committee on Public Utility Economics.
HD2766.R35        363.6'0973        73-21991
ISBN 0-88410-258-0

# Contents

| | |
|---|---|
| List of Figures | ix |
| List of Tables | xi |
| Acknowledgments | xiii |
| List of Contributors | xv |
| Editors' Introduction | 1 |
| Notes to Editors' Introduction | 3 |

**Chapter One**
**Regulation, Entry and Public Enterprise** — 5

| | |
|---|---|
| Entry | 5 |
| Public Enterprise | 6 |
| Both "Utilities" and Regulation Evolve | 6 |
| Alternative Types of Entry | 11 |
| Public Enterprise | 15 |
| Next Steps | 22 |
| Notes to Chapter One | 23 |
| References | 24 |

**Chapter Two**
**Regulatory Reform** — 27

| | |
|---|---|
| Introduction | 27 |
| A Digression on Taxicabs | 30 |
| Expectations | 34 |

## vi Contents

| | |
|---|---|
| Concluding Remarks | 39 |
| Notes to Chapter Two | 40 |

### Chapter Three
### A Critique of Regulatory Accommodation to Change — 41

| | |
|---|---|
| Introduction | 41 |
| Conflicting Pressures and Change Under Regulation | 42 |
| Three Case Studies | 43 |
| Barriers to Successful Accommodation | 55 |
| Toward a Positive Program for Improvement | 57 |
| Notes to Chapter Three | 60 |

### Chapter Four
### The Averch-Johnson Hypothesis after Ten Years — 67

| | |
|---|---|
| Developments in the Theory | 67 |
| Empirical Evidence | 69 |
| Further Directions for Empirical Analysis | 75 |
| References to Chapter Four | 78 |

### Chapter Five
### Perspectives on CATV Regulation — 79

| | |
|---|---|
| Public Policy in Broadcasting | 79 |
| Supply Functions | 80 |
| FCC Regulation of CATV to 1970 | 82 |
| Why Was the FCC Hostile? | 84 |
| Enter New Forces | 85 |
| FCC Regulation, 1972 | 86 |
| Multiple Government Regulation | 88 |
| Concluding Comments | 89 |
| References to Chapter Five | 90 |

### Chapter Six
### Reversals in Peak and Offpeak Prices — 93

| | |
|---|---|
| Introduction | 93 |
| The Profit Versus the Welfare Objective | 94 |
| The Regulated Firm | 99 |
| Two-Part Tariffs | 103 |
| Summary | 108 |
| Notes to Chapter Six | 108 |
| References | 110 |

### Chapter Seven
### A Method for Setting Norms in Regulated Industries ... 113

A Proposed Norm ... 114
Regulatory Policies and "Mix and Share" ... 115
Continuous Surveillance ... 115
Incentives and Evaluation with Respect to Mix and Share ... 116
Identification of Problem Areas ... 117
Summary ... 119
Notes to Chapter Seven ... 123

### Chapter Eight
### Why Regulate Utilities? ... 125

Notes to Chapter Eight ... 135

**Index** ... 137

**About the Authors** ... 139

# List of Figures

| | | |
|---|---|---|
| 5-1 | Supply Curves of Television Channels in a Community | 81 |
| 6-1 | Welfare Versus Monopoly Pricing | 98 |
| 6-2 | Increasing Returns to Capacity | 99 |
| 6-3 | Pricing under Rate-of-Return Regulation | 102 |
| 6-4 | Two-Part Tariff and Rate-of-Return Regulation | 106 |
| 6-5 | Pricing with Limited Customer Charge | 107 |

# List of Tables

| | | |
|---|---|---|
| 1-1 | Stages of Utility Life-Cycle | 7 |
| 1-2 | Selected Public-Enterprise Activities in the United States | 17 |
| 6-1 | Summary of Results | 96 |
| 7-1 | Operating Revenue per Telephone | 120 |
| 7-2 | Numerical Components of Operating Revenue per Telephone | 121 |

# Acknowledgments

We wish to thank the Inter-University Committee on Public Utility Economics for sponsoring the conference at which most of the papers in this volume were presented. The Committee's program is funded by the Michigan Bell Telephone Company, but with no strings or influence attached. We also thank the Committee's Chairman, Dean William Haber, for his encouragement and advice.

For permission to reprint various parts of what follows, we are indebted to the editors of the *American Economic Review*, the *Bell Journal of Economics and Management Science*, and the *Journal of Law and Economics*.

# List of Contributors

William G. Shepherd, Professor of Economics, University of Michigan.
Thomas G. Gies, Professor of Finance, Graduate School of Business Administration, University of Michigan.
Donald J. Dewey, Professor of Economics, Columbia University.
Harry M. Trebing, Professor of Economics, and Director of the Institute of Public Utilities, Michigan State University.
Leland L. Johnson, Manager, Communications Policy Program, the Rand Corporation.
Harold J. Barnett, Professor of Economics, Washington University.
Elizabeth E. Bailey, Adjunct Assistant Professor of Economics, New York University, and Bell Telephone Laboratories.
Lawrence J. White, Assistant Professor of Economics, Princeton University.
Barbara B. Murray, Associate Professor of Economics, University of Detroit.
Harold Demsetz, Professor of Economics, University of California at Los Angeles.

# Editors' Introduction

The revival of serious discontent and of research on public regulation in the 1960s has now bred several specialties:

1. Cost-benefit estimation of regulation's effects. The background question: are there net benefits, and under what conditions?
2. Analysis of technical points, especially of inducements to investment. Younger specialists have found the Averch-Johnson hypothesis (see Chapter Four) particularly attractive.
3. Reform-oriented evaluations. These conventional studies try to show how present regulation can be improved without much change in the structure.
4. Nihilism from Chicago. A series of studies has endeavored to show that regulation is, and must be, irrelevant or pernicious.

The new thought and research already amounts to a devastating indictment of regulation as possibly an intractable vehicle of waste and deception.

Yet it seems that regulation thrives on adversity. It is forty years since Henry Simons branded it the worst of both worlds, thirty-three years since Horace Gray urged that it had been proven unfit, and fifteen years since Meyer, Peck, Stenason and Zwick advanced a powerful case for deregulating the railroads.[1] Yet regulation is still firmly in place and even spreading to new sectors. The "crisis in regulation" seems to be a permanent one, or perhaps a phony one.

Evidently regulation has deep roots, and perhaps the alternatives to it are less promising than many of us, in the heat of criticism, have hoped. There *must* be a better way, we know; but what is it? That is one direction for creative work in the future. Another is to trace those roots, to see why regulation is so stubbornly viable even as it evolves seemingly in the wrong directions. A third is to reassess what regulation really is doing; is it a set of economic constraints, a charade, or possibly a safety valve for discontent, as Donald Dewey suggests below?

More rethinking and research on regulation can help us understand the little engine, even though it seems incapable of changing or redirecting it. Therefore, papers of the sort conveyed by this volume are important for understanding regulation. Eventually, of course, the process of rethinking and research may succeed in changing regulation after all, and in the right directions. It is self-interest and the social images of reality which ultimately create or destroy public policies. By clarifying the self-interests and advancing new images of regulation and its alternatives, we are laying the indispensable basis—necessary even if not sufficient—for change.

In this context, these papers try to offer a balanced sample of current thinking. Most of them are from a conference of economists held in October, 1972. We have added two other papers which, in our judgment, add provocative hypotheses.[2] The upshot is a wide variety of viewpoints and technical levels, touching on many of the recent and coming issues in the field.

Naturally there is no common viewpoint. But all of thinking in this book is, we believe, animated by the kind of skeptical objectivity which regulation, like any other social device, must sustain. Deep down, we must all wish that regulation is actually working tolerably well or can be made to do so. Otherwise its continued presence would scarcely be tolerable. Still, if it does not work well, or cannot, we can gain by clarifying the alternatives.

At the start, one of the Editors places the evaluation of regulation, and proposals for de-regulation and public enterprise, in a context of industry life-cycle. As utilities change and mature, the optimum policy treatments for them also evolve. The key objective should be to get the policy choice right for new utility sectors; and here the possibilities are rich. By contrast, classical public enterprise in old utility sectors is an idea whose time has—in the main—come *and* gone.

Next Donald J. Dewey tells us that regulation is not what it traditionally is believed to be: a lid on profits, or a complex set of economic constraints, or a vehicle for public knowledge. It is just an escape valve for social discontent, a forum where people can at least have their say. And none the worse for that, says Dewey; the value of easing social strain is great.

Harry M. Trebing then outlines basic reasons for a frequent inability of regulation to adjust to change. Detailed lessons are drawn from experience in communications, natural gas, and the postal service (the last a regulated public firm).

Leland L. Johnson takes a ten-year retrospect on the celebrated Averch-Johnson hypothesis. The hypothesis has not been disproved, he finds, but its reach is modest and its validity may ultimately not be testable. If so, the way is open for later twenty-year and thirty-year retrospects, and even an Averch-Johnson Jubilee in 2012, perhaps mounted by economists yet unborn.

In Chapter Five, Harold J. Barnett traces the tortuous borning of cable TV and appraises the new FCC policies. On what may become a major new "utility," Barnett offers erudition plus realism.

Chapters Six and Seven explore rather more technical points. The old but basic question of marginal-cost pricing is re-analyzed creatively by Elizabeth E. Bailey and Lawrence J. White. This topic needs continual refreshing, for it is at the heart of utility pricing policy. It is either the standard to meet or the reference point from which specific departures may be justified. Barbara B. Murray then presents a method of analyzing and predicting revenues from a variety of services. Such techniques may help regulation anticipate problems, rather than just react to them.

Finally, Harold Demsetz asks "Why Regulate Utilities" at all? This paper has become something of a classic and should be read by those (there are many) who believe that if an industry can be classified as a "utility," it should be regulated in the good old way.

Part of the vigor of these papers arises from the direct participation of some of the authors in what they are writing about. Johnson, for example, created at least half of Averch-Johnson and is a leading expert on the telecommunications. Trebing has been deeply engaged in actual proceedings, with the FCC and the Postal Rate Commission. Barnett has been a leading critic of FCC policies toward cable TV. And so with the other writers, in varying degree. If wisdom can be gained both in the fray and in the study, perhaps this collection contains it.

**NOTES**

1. Henry C. Simons, "A Positive Program for Laissez-Faire," 1934, reprinted in his *Economic Policy for a Free Society*. University of Chicago Press, 1949, esp. p. 51; Horace M. Gray, "The Passing of the Public Utility Concept," *Journal of Land and Public Utility Economics*, February 1940; and J.M. Meyer, M.J. Peck, J. Stenason and C. Zwick, *The Economics of Competition in the Transportation Industries*, Harvard Economic Studies, Harvard University Press, 1959.

2. We have also borrowed part of our title from Niel Bernstein's "Utility Rate Regulation: The Little Locomotive that Couldn't," *Washington University Law Quarterly*, Summer 1970.

Chapter One

# Regulation, Entry and Public Enterprise

William G. Shepherd

This paper will consider: 1. why regulation appears to need "reform," 2. whether "de-regulation" and increased entry by new competitors will suffice to reform it, and 3. what role public enterprise might also play in new policy experiments. My theme will be that entry and public enterprise do have their uses, but these uses differ from the usual proposals. At the least, they may do more good than most other ideas for "reforming" regulation.*

**Entry.**
As criticism of regulation has grown in recent years, entry has become a favorite direction for reform. In railroads, telephones, banking, television, stock markets, postal service, even electricity, entry is occurring, imminent, or reasonably possible. This has paralleled the emergence of entry and barriers as main topics in the broader industrial organization literature.

Yet the scope and varieties of entry under regulation have not been studied in depth, nor related to the normal evolution of utility markets. In trying to define the optimum regulatory treatment of entry, therefore, we have only general platitudes and *ad hoc* details. I will suggest that entry poses more difficult and fundamental questions for regulation than we commonly recognize.

The key to the topic is the regulatory contract. This contract, often by custom rather than explicit clauses, governs competition. I will suggest that the contract is more freakish than has been realized, because it contains a series of absolute exclusions. These usually conflict with the routine evolution of the "utility" and of the optimum policy treatment for it. Our task for the next two decades is to rewrite the regulatory contract further, to return it to normal con-

---

*Portions of this paper appeared in "Entry as a Substitute for Regulation," *American Economic Review*, May 1973, and "Public Enterprise," a chapter in R. Nader and M.J. Green, eds., *Corporate Power in America*, Grossman, 1972.

tractual conditions of specific duties and penalties. Some of this will undo policy work of the 1930s, and earlier, which is now obsolete.

**Public Enterprise.**
As for public enterprise, it is important to bring it into any appraisal of public regulation. Public enterprise can be a versatile supplement to regulation, as well as—in some cases—a partial alternative to it.

Yet we often mistakenly equate public enterprise with just one narrow stereotype of it: the classic British public corporation, a monopoly, funded by the Treasury, in a utility sector, and perhaps with big social impacts. The TVA is also in this mold. This old-fashioned public enterprise does not have to earn profits, nor pay taxes. It gets capital at below-market rates, and it absorbs more capital than is optimal. That is the standard image we have all been accustomed to apply to public enterprise. It has been familiar both in old political debates and in the more technical literature.[1]

But there is much more to it. I will offer three lessons: First, public enterprise as a tool should be judged objectively by its costs and benefits, like any other policy tool. Second, public enterprise comes in many forms, varieties and degrees. Some of these are effective, some are very costly. The familiar public corporation, British style, is a very narrow set of those possibilities. Third, in utility sectors we have too little of the more experimental types of public enterprise and possibly too much of the conventional public corporation.

In short, we will cover the new major alternative to regulation—entry and deregulation—and the old, old one—public enterprise. First, in Section One, we have to understand why regulation may go wrong. Entry is taken up in Section Two and public enterprise in Section Three.

My hypotheses concern the utility life-cycle, the regulatory contract, and the reverse evolution of regulation. I will first offer a series of brief propositions, and then consider four types of entry.

### 1. Both "Utilities" and Regulation Evolve.

**1. "Utility sectors" commonly proceed through four stages.** To judge the prospects for entry, we need first to recall what might be entered and why. A regulated utility is usually a *system* providing many services to a spectrum of users whose levels and elasticities of demand vary greatly. The network has permanence, often uses public facilities, and is often attached physically to the user. The utility's technology can change or be supplanted by rival modes.

Most utilities can be said to pass through four stages, as follows (in skeleton form). In *Stage 1*, the system is inverted, often leading to control by patents. This stage is usually brief but decisive for the form of the system. *Stage 2* is system creation and growth, often displacing a prior "utility." Cross-subsidies among users and a separation of creamy and skim markets become embedded in the price structure. The new service seeks regulated status for permanence, legitimacy and market control; and the regulators act as promoters to make the service available to all households.

In *Stage 3* the system becomes complete as a matter of technology and market saturation. It now shifts from offense to defense. Competing new technologies arise, beyond the utility's control, to substitute for it in basic and peripheral markets. Physical layout and pricing structure do not fit evolving city patterns as well as before. Users in lucrative markets challenge the prices they face, and traditional external impacts (e.g., pollution of eye, ear, nose, throat, and of regulatory hearings) are less acceptable. The utility more and more finds itself trying to obstruct new technology or to warp it to fit its private optimum structure. Finally, in *Stage 4*, the systemic monopoly attributes yield to these pressures of competition and technology; and the sector reverts—no longer a "utility"—to conventional competitive processes. Or, in certain cases, where externalities and equity are peculiarly important, a public enterprise solution is superior.

Table 1-1 estimates very roughly the stages for a number of present and past "utilities." During these stages the technology prescribes different optimum structures and policy treatments.

2. **Regulation usually starts in Stage 2, in harmony with the interests of the utility and its larger industrial customers.** The structure of mutual interests, the profit expectations and the terms of exchange (the rate level and structure) therefore precede regulation, as in railroads, electricity, telephones, banks, and now the Postal Service. Regulation then legitimizes, reinforces, and smooths these interest-group compromises—Webster's definition of "regulation,"

**Table 1-1. Stages of Utility Life-Cycle: Approximate Intervals**

|  | *Stage 1* | *Stage 2* | *Stage 3* | *Stage 4* |
|---|---|---|---|---|
| Manufactured gas | 1800-1820 | 1820-1880 | 1880-1920 | 1920-1950 |
| Natural gas | 1900-1910 | 1910-1950 | 1950- |  |
| Telegraph | 1840-1850 | 1850-1916 | 1916-1930 | 1930- |
| Railways: All | 1820-1835 | 1835-1910 |  |  |
|     Passenger |  |  | 1910-1935 | 1935- |
|     Freight |  |  | 1910-1960 | 1960- |
| Electricity | 1870-1885 | 1885-1960 | 1960- |  |
| Street railways | 1870-1885 | 1885-1912 | 1912-1922 | 1922- |
| Telephone | 1875-1880 | 1880-1947 | 1947- |  |
| Airlines | 1920-1925 | 1925-1965 | 1965- |  |
| Television | 1935-1947 | 1947-1965 | 1965- |  |
| Cable TV | 1950-1955 | 1955- |  |  |

number two: "to reduce to order . . . to regularize." It can alter them—definition one: "to govern or direct according to rule"—only marginally. (Often only Oxford definition number four applies: "to make regulations"). Rate structure is never thoroughly assessed and changed. If commissions were converted into Utility Advisory Boards—to define what utilities and major customers should do to protect their long-run interests, to legitimize their acts, and to avert reductions in share prices—their behavior would be little changed. Regulation does use honorific terms and rituals that have lulled academics, which explains why their disillusion with what is perceived as the Dream Factory now runs deep. To doubt that 45 of 50 state commissions, and 7 of 10 federal ones, constrain matters of economic substance—except possibly the prospects for public enterprise—one needs only look closely and skeptically at their resources, behavior and results.

Therefore, as it were by contract, regulation promotes and protects the utility and its larger customers on into Stages 3 and 4.

**3. Regulation has (barring the odd exception) inadequate funds and mediocre talent for its supposed economic tasks.** Those at its center have little motivation, or even understanding, to change the basic contract and the process.

**4. The contract excludes seller competition from the service area, in exchange for a review process. The efficacy of the review atrophies, from lack of funds, expertise and powers. The exclusions spread and become absolute.** The contract is formally with utility owners, and it often becomes a large equity value in Stage 3. But its key effects are on managers. The exclusions protect management from evaluation, control, or takeover. Few managements, ever, can have been so privileged and so isolated. They (and their boards—usually passive) occupy a strange position between shareholders and commission. What, if anything, they are maximizing is unclear. Such a vacuum has attracted theorists, but it leaves incentives and responsibility—and the public interest—in limbo.

Managers find it natural to maximize along both dimensions of profitability: (1) the rate of return (by influencing commission as well as company behavior), and (2) risk-avoidance (by maximizing their present and future market shares). Since profit rates are formally limited, the firm satisfices by devoting resources (or sacrificed profits) instead to market-share-maintaining activities of many kinds, including some noted by Averch-Johnson. This activity differs from non-pecuniary maximizing (translate: waste) and is probably larger in total resource loss. Formal profit limits, therefore, induce hyper-control of the market and hyper-reaction against new entry. The franchise and regulatory processes themselves are among the instruments with which managers maximize the utility's value and minimize managerial uncertainty; and since the utility's share prices capitalize the value of the franchise, any threat to their value—such as by unilateral new entry—is "confiscation," and *ergo* intolerable to the regulators.

In this way regulation is non-neutral toward entry; the bias arises from the contract, and it is accentuated by the profit constraints. This bias further increases the utility's bargaining power against the commission: the utility, being irreplaceable, must be propitiated. So regulation tends toward stable corner solutions on entry, preventing it entirely. That may be appropriate for Stage 2, but it is not for Stages 3 and 4.

5. **The contract de facto allots responsibility and service liability in large part, and increasingly, to the commission.** Penalties and rewards are not applied—either in general or specific directions—to utility performance. Instead of asserting or imposing the public interest, the commission ultimately accepts service responsibility. Under it, too—and this is perhaps the crowning oddity—there are no practical, specific penalties on the utility for specific non-fulfillments (e.g., outages, crossed wires, late planes) or for general failures of management. The contract lacks explicit performance standards, and it is devoid of mechanisms for enforcing any possible standards. The only penalties are political, and these hurt the regulators as much as the utilities. The utility's and commission's objective therefore becomes simply to minimize political repercussions, to avoid redressing inequities, to gloss over. The strangeness of the managers' role is matched only by that of the regulators'.

6. So the contract hyper-excludes:

   a. It excludes seller entry from primary markets and often even from secondary and tertiary ones.
   b. It excludes inter-area competition for major customers.
   c. It excludes takeover or any lesser change in managerial and financial control, either by private interests or ultimately by the commission itself or other public groups.
   d. It excludes product-liability claims by legitimate plaintiffs.
   e. It excludes rivalrous innovation, of Schumpeterian or other types.
   f. It excludes regulatory choices which would cause significant reductions in utility share prices.
   g. It excludes thorough, neutral treatments of third-party effects of utility actions (e.g., on the environment).
   h. And it excludes future revisions or termination of the contract itself.

Taken together, these exclusions are of extraordinary scope and permanence. Few of these exclusions, and their likely costs, are clearly recognized for what they are. The contract breeds mutual vested interests against change, even among potential entrants. In short, there is a *reversed evolution* of regulation, in the opposite direction from what utility evolution calls for.

## 10  Regulation in Further Perspective

**7. This contract, by removing constraints, induces inefficiencies of several sorts.** The new demonology of regulation has not fixed the relative importance of these costs, nor, probably, will it ever do so precisely. My appraisal is that the three leading costs are:

   a. Internal Inefficiency. Railroads and, more recently, electric and telephone companies are partial examples.
   b. A greater degree of exclusivity in utility technology, which induces innovation below optimal levels and in non-optimal directions. This may be largest in telephones and electricity (see Capron, Kahn, Phillips).
   c. Excess peak demand and capacity induced by non- and anti-marginalist price structures (see Shepherd, 1966). It took us and Samuel Insull a long time to get promotional rates to explore demand elasticity and scale frontiers. Now, in many utility services, the opposite marginal conditions arise and require reversing the price structures to fit true costs and to abate peak demand.

A-J effects may be present in all three costs, but they alone are not the main problem. Also, as Kahn notes, A-J may fit long-run optimizing not fight it.

We have clearly come light years since the 1930s, when Leo Sharfman could take the ICC at face value, with admiration. Nor is regulation merely a Transylvanian drama, picaresque but trivial, as the Chicago muses tell us. It applies and masks powerful economic influences. The mass of economically aware regulators (perhaps a small mass) must lead lives of quiet desperation. And even if economists were to replace lawyers in running the Dream Factory, most of the costs would still probably occur. There would be too few alert, forceful Brethren, perhaps for only the federal commissions, and the contract would be unchanged.

These costs are insidious because they are piecemeal, difficult to detect, and *officially* not to be permitted or admitted. (Ask any regulator how much inefficiency he/she permits.) They often increase utility and commission security from breakdowns (this is one A-J effect), and so they can be said to provide "high-quality" service even if they are wasteful. They are inaccessible to any "incentive regulation" yet designed. There is also little inherent pressure from regulation toward equity, to protect poor, politically weak users from being overcharged relative to wealthy powerful ones (example: the pricing of electricity to center-city and suburban groups). These costs are likely to increase during Stage 3. The normal constraints on management are off, and the utility's incentives are to tighten the exclusions further.

**8. The exclusions tend to be stable and homeostatic.** Seller entry is difficult to force unilaterally upon a utility. Any such severe depressant on utility stock prices is "confiscatory." Moreover, large firms are commonly reluctant to try to enter, probably because their other profit opportunities exceed those which regulation formally permits. In addition, as in the classic Western Electric instance, both sides mutually fear new competition. Small entrants are vulnerable and usually of trivial effect. Attempts at "better" regulation of rates—hiring more brilliant commissioners or staffs, giving them bigger budgets—does not correct the basic structural problems or the inefficiencies.

### 2. Alternative Types of Entry

The upshot is anti-Darwinian with a vengeance: regulation is ill-fitted from the start, evolves the wrong way to fit its proper economic function, and survives only too well. Abolition is usually too simple and abrupt an answer, except for Stage 4 cases. A different contractual basis, rather, is needed, plus a routine sequence of steps treating competition.

For "entry," I presently perceive four main directions. Some of them may be able to resolve the serious problems into which our present Stage 3 "regulated utilities" have slipped.

**1. New seller entry.** This term is now what is usually meant by "entry" (example: Carterfone and MCI vs. the Bell System). Upwards of 70 years ago, J.B. Clark pointed out that potential competition could neutralize even a pure monopoly position. To matter at all, potential must credibly threaten to become actual; and entry must be easy. Still, the concept clearly had merit for evaluating individual monopolists. In the 1930s, Edward Chamberlin altered the context to an oligopoly basis, on which it is still set. The operative concepts were now the leading-firm group and the market boundary, across which entry by new firms might occur.

In this industry context, Joe Bain then advanced the concept of the "barrier" against entry. Barriers are said to arise from scale economies, product differentiation, patents, capital costs, and other factors. Entry is made by new firms creating new capacity. The scope of this entry is defined first by the new share taken and second by the speed of the entry. (I should add the degree of surprise, in defining entry; expected entry differs in impact from unexpected entry.) The height of the barrier, it is argued, then governs—more closely even than do market shares or oligopoly concentration—the pricing strategy and profit chances of the leading firms.

These familiar truths became conventional in the 1960s; but they are now entering a period of revision, as all popular ideas must. For regulation, the main lessons of it all are three, briefly put: (1) Entry is rarely distinct, in theory or in practice, from other structural changes (e.g., small-firm growth or oligopolists' strategies toward each other); (2) The probability of entry is inverse to its scope. Major entry is a rarity, and is, therefore, normally a second-order decision variable; (3) The impact of entry occurs via changes in the established firm's market share.

These doubts about the importance of entry are reinforced by recent econometric tests covering a large number of large United States industrial firms (see also Shepherd, 1972): (1) The market share of the firm, *not* barriers to its industry, appears to be the main structural determinant of profit rates; (2) Only when barriers are reduced all the way down to "low" levels are profit rates significantly reduced; (3) Barrier height is not related, simply or partially, to the degree of stability of market shares. Finally, among all the postwar changes in United States industrial markets, major entry is rather a rarity; and in almost every case it occurs slowly, with little surprise, and comes from large firms in related markets. In many major industries—the pathological market-power cases—it does not happen at all, despite high profit rates of the established firms, often for decades. Entry succeeds mainly when the prior firms are unusually slow-moving. Alert monopolists who can price-discriminate normally can head off significant entry (examples: IBM, United Shoe Machinery). Much of the observed postwar entry has in fact been arranged by the federal government (synthetic rubber, aluminum) or by public enterprises.

The upshot: for new-seller entry to take much effect, market share must go down soon and far, toward 70 or 50 percent or even lower, and remain down. Technology must be readily available to entrants, and prior firms must be unable to use price discrimination to avert entry. Actually most utilities can discriminate sharply, even under regulation; and many do. Recall again that regulated utilities are uniquely insulated. Entrants are vulnerable and resistance to them is magnified; the seeming paranoia of utilities, to whom every entrant is the thin edge of a large wedge, is a natural result of this insulation.

If regulators merely try to stand aside and passively permit seller entry, little will happen. Regulators will need to help make entry happen, and to keep entry open for further new entrants. Short of total deregulation, entry makes the regulatory task more complex, not less. (Deregulation makes the *antitrust* problem *more* complex.)

Is such new entry conceivable in regulated utility markets? Hardly, for if it is effective, it lowers expected returns and share prices, and thereby threatens regulation itself. Experience is equally bearish. In the telephone industry prospective new entry is only peripheral and slow, despite the carriers' alarmist assertions. Among electric companies new sellers are far less promising than existing ones (see 3 below). A moderate seller entry policy may be the least rewarding of all worlds: the profit inducements for entry are modest; it is technologically difficult; it unambiguously reduces carrier opportunities; and so it will be resisted even to the point of congesting regulatory processes. It is probably the least promising direction for entry policy. It conflicts with the regulatory contract, rather than revising it; it violates settled interests rather than redirecting them.

2. **Entry to the managerial and supervisory functions.** The regulatory contract has provided virtual carte blanche for managers and their boards,

with results which—in other more normal sectors—would provoke waves of takeovers and managerial changes. Utilities are, with one or two exceptions, perfectly amenable—in size, simplicity of technology and profit opportunities—to takeover or partial shifts of control. Only regulation stands in the way, anxious to assure service at virtually any cost.

The proper solution is straightforward: write specific service criteria and liability standards into the contract, and then permit nearly any ownership or managerial change. Many service liabilities would be insurable. As for ownership changes, in the electric industry this would require revising the Public Utility Act of 1935 to permit all—or perhaps only certain categories of—nonutility firms to own utility ones. Their operations and accounts would of course be kept separate. The Act has served much of its original purpose, but now it shields management and protects inefficiency, as does the Bank Holding Company Act of 1968, which neatly protects large banks from takeover. For such actual or potential entry to operate, a large share of each utility's (and subsidiaries') stock needs to be out in the market, so that independent ownership exists and can operate to check management performance. For telephone and electric utilities, this would require releasing at least 49 percent of the stock of major subsidiaries, both operating and supplying. Such a shift will assure accountability, by keeping the books separate and subject to the markets' evaluation. Performance would no longer be buried in hierarchy.

Nearly all such utility units are not forbiddingly large or complex. There are other large enterprises capable of perceiving, and of acting to correct, inefficiencies in utilities. These improvements require changed behavior, not necessarily drastic personnel shifts. The last decade of mergers has shown that takeovers commonly fail either when the aggressor firm is smaller and younger than its target and can be discredited for unreliability, or when the target firm can invoke a public agency to protect it.

Regulators, therefore, would need to take great care to be neutral to takeover, lest they unwittingly stop it cold. If strict neutrality is maintained, past experience suggests that active, diverse, effective—and thoroughly normal— constraints on utility management would appear at long last. Commissions cannot be expected to monitor or change managerial performance, even if they were to try, as I suggested years ago that they do (Trebing). The market might do it; if not, public entry and ownership—partial or complete— may be more effective. At present, the potential for unperceived and uncorrectable inefficiency is high, and takeover access—plus clear service liability—will reach it more directly than conventional regulation or new seller entry can.

**3. Revision of existing sellers.** Regulated firms commonly provide a variety of separable services, with differing elasticities of demand and degrees of competition. These can be separated, for accountability. At present, regulation permits finances to be over-combined and market structure to be kept more rigid than necessary, especially in Stage 3. This is true now of banking, air transport, communications, electric power, and combination electric and gas firms, among others.

Instead, structure should be changeable, and in some fields the separation and realignment of activities should be routinely permitted. In banking, for example, key personnel responsible for key clients should be able to leave and form separate firms—new "entrants" from within, as it were—using their special skills. This "entry" by realignment would be far more effective than entry by new banks could be. In communications, experts and managers to form new competitive entities could come from *within* the existing carriers—as many of IBM's small competitors have—were it not for traditional and regulatory rules which require franchises. In electric power, customer groups—including whole cities (such as Elbow Lake, Minnesota) or other commercial users—could be formed to pool demand and take over distribution directly, much more commonly than is now occurring. Independent distribution would then exist within the formerly monolithic service areas. Such revisions would apply skilled inside talent, rather than vulnerable outsiders. The key provision is, again, having explicit service liability standards, so that regulators need not evaluate the fitness of suppliers.

4. **Inter-area competition.** There are new opportunities for competition among carriers in each others' "service areas." Bulk electricity supply markets have now become the best example of this, but they are not the only one. A range of regulatory changes is possible in treating these, but they all amount finally to letting utilities bid customers away from other utilities. This, too, simply restores normal economic behavior.

Where technology permits such a mingling of supply relationships—as it does in bulk electricity—the gains could be large. Inefficiency would be under direct constraint, for the first time in generations (pun intended). Service standards and cheapness would both be used to gain customers, as they should be; this would ease the probable present bias toward excessive service "quality." Utilities would be induced to develop and use the technology of large scale supply more fully.

The change could offer net gains to many utilities, since it widens their opportunities. It is bilateral, not a unilateral threat to managerial security and share values. Therefore it could dissolve, or at least reduce, the balkanized homeostasis which now prevails. Possibly it would be welcomed, not resisted, by utilities.

In bulk electric power, the possibilities are quite good. Though Leonard Weiss has explored them (see Phillips), nobody has been out in the trenches working for them more than James R. Nelson. Throughout the country, many hundreds of major customers are within range of alternative suppliers and presumably would seek bids. Some are cities, such as Elbow Lake, again, and Gainesville, Florida, now in a test case. Others are large private firms. In Michigan, for example, about one-third of the largest commercial accounts at single locations are close enough to alternative suppliers to take bids, even if wheeling were not required. If wheeling were mandatory, the fraction would be much higher. Other industrial areas are similar.

Although full-blown inter-area competition would only affect the larger customers, many smaller users could pool their demand. It would naturally introduce complex game conditions into the present rigidity. Pooling and mergers would become strategic elements in the process, since many adjoining utilities would be both competing and cooperating. Some among us might fear that intolerable discrimination, and possibly collusion, would result. I would prefer that we try it first, as a learning experience. The sector is not more complex or prone to natural monopoly than are many "competitive" markets in the industrial sector. The efficiency gains could be large, and there is already much discrimination and absolute non-competition in the patchwork we have now.

The basic revision in the regulatory contract is simple: contracts with an "outside" supplier would be unregulated. The rest of the utility's business would remain its "service area" and subject to regulation. Wheeling at reasonable charges—or as part of exchange agreements—would be required, within certain distances. Separate transmission lines could be built at will for outside supply, but—pending more detailed study and experience—possibly not using power of eminent domain. Horizontal mergers which would adversely affect this competition (as most of them would) would require overriding evidence of scale economies. Indeed, many of the larger systems are probably already too large, by this criterion.

The result will be a more complicated and efficient industry. The mass of smaller contracts will still be regulated, but by a stream-lined and focused regulation process. Terms of service and the liability for all service will be explicit. Structure and contracts will be more flexible, in some cases as the outcome of intricate strategy. In short, part of the industry will evolve properly through Stage 3 toward economic normality. A clear parallel is the New York Stock Exchange, where deregulation of large sales has led to highly effective competition.

### 3. Public Enterprise

The cardinal fact about public ownership is that it is not a substitute for regulation. It is rather a substitute—on another plane—for *private* ownership, not for regulation. Wave a wand, convert private utilities to public corporations, and most of the problems of regulation will remain just as before.

Still, public enterprise may supplement other policy choices, and so it merits a detailed look. The first point to recognize is that public enterprises come in a great variety.[2] Let us define public enterprise quite broadly, to include quasi-public enterprises and non-profit enterprises, as well as the older styles. To illustrate the variety:

We are, most of us, born in a public enterprise. Most of us go to school in public enterprises, and possibly we go on to a public college or university. Many of us actually work for public enterprises, as I do at the University of Michigan.

Many people who do not work for public enterprises, ride to and from their work in public-enterprise buses or subways. If they drive their cars, they often park their cars in public-enterprise parking structures.

We are entertained at concerts by publicly-supported orchestras, operas and other performing arts groups, such as university football teams, which provide a form of entertainment. For that matter, many professional baseball, football, hockey, basketball and other teams play in city-owned stadiums.

We go to city, state and national parks. We take off and land from public airports, guided by public air safety systems and weather reporting services. Many people live in public housing.

Others of us are likely to finance the purchase of our house, if we can afford one, with an FHA loan which, of course, is another public enterprise. If we have any money left over for checking and savings deposits, those are insured by the FDIC, which is another public enterprise. Public enterprises handle our mail, our water, part of our electricity, our sewage, and often our garbage. They handle our antiquities, in public museums around the country. If we commit a crime we are perhaps going to be tried in a quasi-public enterprise known as the courts, and we may go to jail, which is another public enterprise.

As and if we enter our golden years, we may visit hospitals which are public enterprises, more frequently than we would really prefer. Our treatment will be paid for by Medicare, a public enterprise, and, of course, we will begin to draw on Social Security, which is another public enterprise. And, finally, we may come to rest in that final public enterprise, the city cemetery.

Among all these different kinds—and there are many others too—some are quite important. They adopt varying economic rules and policies towards us. Some of them we pay for directly, some indirectly. Some of them are in competition with other entities, some of them are monopolies.

Many of the things we value most, and by which we define our culture, are public enterprises. The United States has relatively few of them in the industrial, utility, and financial sectors, compared to other advanced economics; but many important public enterprises in United States utility and financial sectors are little recognized.

The main questions in the present context are whether there should be more or less public enterprise in the utility sector, and what forms it might take. Do utilities have special technology and cost attributes, and are there special benefits which they offer that mark them out for public enterprise? Note also that if regulation has failed as badly as some of my colleagues think, and if a competitive basis for utility behavior is not feasible, then by default public enterprise is the only solution left to try. Public enterprise has two main elements. The first is economic resources provided by the state, for current costs or for capital investment. They include funds, risk-absorption, managerial talent, natural resources. These are scarce resources, which need to be used sparingly. The other main dimension is the degree of public control. Public enterprises differ very widely in this direction. Some of them are essentially uncontrolled, literally autonomous, whereas others are very strictly controlled in the interests of the public.[3]

A variety of public enterprises are arrayed in Table 1-2, to show how wide the variety is along these two dimensions. Two other elements are the degree to which the enterprise has a monopoly of its activity, and the degree to which it is a local-based or local-controlled activity.

In most cases the public interest is served by *minimizing* public *sponsorship, maximizing* public *control*, and *maximizing* the degree of *competition* and of *local control.* Generally, cases toward the upper left of Table 1-2 give higher yields than those in the lower right (many offer social benefits much smaller than their social costs). Of course, in many cases there must be trade-offs among the elements; but the basic direction of optimal policy is clear.

Our topic therefore leads into all manner of pricing choices, degrees of subsidy or tight budgeting, internal structures, and market positions. In this perspective, Table 1-2 suggests that many public enterprises are dubious in their present form and context, while others may offer very high yields. Moreover, there may be sectors where new public enterprise tactics would be fruitful. We

**Table 1-2. Selected Public-Enterprise Activities in the United States by Approximate Degree of Control and Subsidy**

|  | *Control* | *Partial Control* | *Slight Control* |
|---|---|---|---|
| No subsidy | Municipal utilities (water, sewage) U.S. Government Printing Office Social Security Municipal parking facilities Municipal transit Federal courts Public law programs Child-care programs | State liquor stores National land management Amtrak SBA programs (including minority support) FAA programs Airports AEC enrichment plants Highway construction and maintenance State courts Local courts Federal maritime program Mental hospitals State and local law enforcement agencies Prisons | Port of New York Authority FHA housing program Sports stadiums Tennessee Valley Authority Performing arts centers Public housing Medicare Medicaid Public universities SST program Military R&D contracting Veterans Administration hospitals |
| Full subsidy | Primary education | Corps of Engineers Census Bureau | Weapons purchasing and management |

can learn also by comparing with other modern economies. The main obvious contrasts between the United States and other countries are in utilities, industry, and finance. In these sectors, public firms are more common abroad than here.

One obvious lesson is that "nationalization" and "public ownership," in the classic British and TVA style, are very special cases, *not* representative of the whole. No nationalization exists in any Western economy that is comparable in scale to "nationalization" in the giant United States economy. Abroad, almost all of the largest public firms operate on a regional and local scale by United States standards. Ownership is only one small variant of public enterprise tactics, and it should almost always be kept as low as possible. Another semantic trap is to think that private is "versus" public. In fact, much public enterprise sustains and subsidizes private firms, some of them powerful and rich. And private resistance to public enterprise is often simply a matter of offer prices. Almost every private entity has a price at which it will actively seek conversion to "public" enterprise. In fact, peaceful extensions of public ownership in the past have usually been peaceful *because* they were generous to the former owners.

In deciding whether and how to use public enterprise tactics, we should use good sense. In economic terms, this means that we will estimate the costs and benefits they entail and then choose a combination of them which makes the best use of scarce policy resources. These resources are of several sorts: tax money, the absorption of risks, manager's talent, and natural resources. They are scarce; and they can be, and very often are, wasted on inferior uses. We will, of course, proceed with care, since the social objectives involved are controversial and the data will permit only rough estimates.

The intelligent way to choose is to compare benefits and costs.[4] The benefits will be of three main sorts: 1. Efficiency; the output wrung from inputs, both now and in growth and progress over time, 2. Equity; fairness in the distribution of opportunities, wealth, and income, and 3. Basic social, cultural and political values. One compares among specific treatments, each of which commonly includes a package of tolls, rather than just one. For example, public firms should, wherever possible, be under the antitrust laws. And many public enterprises need to be regulated. More precisely, policy tools—antitrust, regulation, public enterprise—are often complements to each other.

The variety of resources which public enterprise absorbs needs stressing. In Britain, for instance, the public corporations have drawn appreciably on the managerial capabilities of the country. Possibly they have been less of a drain than any other alternative; but, nevertheless, they take talent from other public-sector activities. Also it takes political control; it takes time in Parliament to supervise how, say, the coal industry is being run. That time subtracts from Parliament's, or Congress's, or the City Council's whole fund of attention; and so it strains the supervisory ability of the political process.

In this perspective, one can distinguish several types of public enterprises which have low or negative social yields, and others which are highly positive. First, the negative cases.

The first of these is *sponsorship of activities used mainly by the wealthy.* The variety of these is wide. Obvious examples include many subsidized programs for performing arts, much suburban commuter service (including large parts of the new Amtrak experiment), tax support of university education for children from upper economic levels, and the format of public parks in most towns.[5] The system of justice, in the context of unequal access to legal counsel, can be regarded as a public enterprise with largely a regressive incidence.[6] Reflection will supply other examples. Many of them would not withstand an objective evaluation of their efficiency and regressive incidence. Sharp revisions and cuts would be efficient for many of what are regarded as our finest institutions, in the arts, education, law and the courts.

Second is the syndrome of the *sick industry*, often using enormous amounts of capital and often selling to (and buying from) large private firms. Since the "sickness" is often industry-wide, with severe dislocations which invite a "unified" treatment, the common result is a centralized monopoly financed directly and extensively by the Treasury. The classic form is the United Kingdom public corporations, in coal, steel and railroads. Railroads are, in fact, in this status almost everywhere in the world.[7] Many of the "social" impacts are external to the industry; but governments routinely fail to treat them directly, leaving them as a burden on the public firm, to be met reluctantly by slowing down, closures and by cross-subsidizing the losing parts.[8] The public firm is also routinely prevented from raising its prices—to help "stop inflation"—and it is expected to raise wages rapidly. The main beneficiaries are industrial users and equipment suppliers, a most unneedy lot.[9] The resulting financial losses, redundancy and demoralization in the public firm are then interpreted to discredit all forms of public enterprise. The unnecessary drain from all this on public funds, on public administration talent, and on "socialist" political impetus has been enormous.[10] But the disillusion with public enterprise should lie only on this specific, benighted form of it.

A third type is the *nationwide public firm in a "healthy" utility sector,* such as electric power and telephones. "Health" means that revenues cover costs (often because of excess demand) and that there are few big external effects (such as pollution) or social impacts. Yet these enterprises still absorb vast amounts of capital and administrative talent. The gains are often minor and (e.g., in the United Kingdom telephones) mainly taken by private firms and upper economic groups.[11] TVA's biggest customers include aluminum firms, a far cry from the rural poor. Moreover, the lack of competitive constraints can breed internal inefficiency which is just as great as that which private utilities in the United States, under regulation, are widely believed to suffer.[12] A switch to private bond financing can abate much of the drain on public funds, but the other costs persist and the whole economic and social yields often remain nugatory.

These are categories of public enterprises which perhaps should—on sound economic criteria—be cut back, revised in format, constrained, and put on different pricing and investment policies. Their objectives are often unclear and their use of tools inefficient. Their vices are primarily monopoly, drainage of public funds, regressive pricing, neglect of externalities and rigidity of form. Their benefits go mainly to powerful, unneedy groups.

By contrast "optimal" public enterprises have tight constraints (by competition or budgetary control), minimum use of public funds and talent, a progressive incidence, clear allowances for external effects on ecology and society, and flexibility in arrangements. They are experiments with short lives, not permanent fixtures. The above are platitudes, but they suggest several types of "good" public enterprise tactics.

One is the *public-firm competitor*, with a quarter or less of the market and, in most cases, some mixture of private-public ownership and motivation. It could force improved pricing and efficiency in tight-oligopoly markets. Its takeover threat to firms in other tight-oligopoly markets could indirectly induce better performance in them too.

A second group is the public entity as *countervailer* against any private market power which seems to be beyond other constraints. An obvious instance is the British national health service as a buyer of drugs from private companies. It is paralleled, but only piecemeal, in this country by the Veterans Administration and certain hospital groups.[13] Defense weapons purchases occasionally, but not consistently, are done on this aggressive basis.

Third are activities with high, progressive benefits spread widely throughout society. A downtown public library is the obvious example, as is the provision of good-quality legal services to poor people. Programs stopping contagious disease are another; so is universal primary schooling, if properly structured, and possibly nursery care. The social-critic and innovator aspects of public universities also are of this sort.

Fourth are units whose outputs go mainly to upper-wealth groups *and which maximize profits.* Prime possible examples are state universities, performing arts programs, and high quality medical care, *if they were properly priced.* This can be done by using price discrimination—charging what the traffic will bear—on a means test or some other basis.

Between these best and worst extremes lie many mixed cases. For example, the Social Security insurance enterprise yields certain high benefits. But its financing is strongly and unnecessarily regressive, a clear defect. Hospital and health-insurance enterprises (Medicare, Medicaid, others) are notoriously lax toward inefficiency. Public housing projects have had obvious bad effects—via isolation and poor design—which could probably be avoided. The three vast AEC uranium-enrichment plants absorb large amounts of public capital and subsidize a very narrow group of large firms and utilities which use their services. In these and other cases, it is the policies which are wrong, not the fact of public enterprise.

The lesson is that there is a great deal of room for experimentation, with new forms of public enterprise. This is distinct from the old public corporation, TVA, the Corps of Engineers, the massive old-fashioned monopoly public enterprise. Yet this degree of possible experimentation is much greater in the manufacturing sector than in the utility sector. In short, we should screen and cut public sponsorship of public corporations in utility sectors which sell primarily to industry and to wealthy people. Much of the Federal power effort is in this category, much of the Federal Housing Authority, and AMTRAK, plus some postal services.

An additional or alternative strategy is simply to switch the enterprise to the private capital markets for securing investment funds. In fact, this is occurring for some of the public corporations in Britain, and it has already occurred for many public firms in this country.

These general points can be focused on two specific sectors, railroads and electricity.

Many of the eastern railroads are now widely believed to be heading, or backing, towards nationalization as the outcome of traffic, management and pricing problems. The most likely process is that the United States Government will be put in the position of guaranteeing the securities of these failing railroads, after the managements themselves have passed the point of salvaging the railroads' finances. Ultimately the government may be left to pay off the bondholders in part or whole and to take over the management. This would involve a very high cost and, typically, a relatively small degree of public control, because the railroads would still be run largely as railroads, for primarily an economic function. Even under public enterprise the railroads would still be carrying their usual traffic, except that now taxpayers would help pay for the process. It would also tend to be on the old monopoly lines, and it would also tend to be not locally-oriented but in large systems.

Such a tendency would in all probability be far from optimal. It would be the classic case of the Government being forced into bailing out a sick industry, for the benefit mainly of large private customers. This is just the opposite of the positive potential of public enterprise to operate in high productivity sectors. The more efficient solution would be to let the private capital markets sort out the insolvent railroads much as they treat any failing private enterprise. At the most, we might find it advisable to have perhaps partial public ownership of certain railroads if there is continued public interest in their management and the specific services they provide. But working control adequate to achieve that effect would usually be possible with only 20 percent of the shares, or possibly less. So at the most, the Government or a set of State governments might get partly into owning and supervising certain railroads which especially affect the public interest. Such promising experiments have not been tried in the past. For example, the Long Island Railroad and others have been transferred all the way into completely public firms, apparently because it has been felt that they must be either entirely private or entirely public. The interesting in-between possibilities have not been explored. To neglect them now would risk a vast federal investment (upwards of $40 billion) and management effort, which could yield scanty returns.

I turn now briefly to the electric power industry. As we saw in Section 2, there are new opportunities for competition among electricity suppliers in each others' "service areas." There is also a significant possible new role for public enterprise in the most basic parts of the system. In regions where mergers with large scale economies would do away with inter-area bulk supply competition, or have already done so, the case for public bulk power network, on the lines of the British Electricity Board of 1926-48, would be very strong. This is the main possible new role I see for public enterprise in this sector.

A national grid would not only enable better coordination; it would also preserve some of the possibilities for competition among suppliers for bulk customers. The grid would be a common carrier, freely willing to wheel or otherwise facilitate rivalry and new entry in a wide range of former service areas. To this extent it would both substitute for some regulation and complement regulatory efforts to constrain prices and inefficiency. It need not be totally publicly owned; a joint-venture or related form would be at least as feasible as a monolithic federally-funded public grid.

In any case, utility sectors offer new possibilities for imaginative uses of public enterprise that have scarcely been perceived so far. The range of devices is large. There also are real doubts about the benefit-cost yields from many of the classic cases of public enterprise in utility sectors. These all add up to a fascinating set of alternatives for study and trial, a true frontier for research. If we can shed the old blinkers of ideology, it may be possible to design and try these tools rationally.

In short, we should explore alternatives *other* than the conventional "nationalized industry," in order to use public resources sparingly but also with real potency.

### 4. Next Steps

To many of us, regulation is like growing old: we would rather not do it, but consider the alternative. From this cleft stick, some observers have come to see entry and competition as a ready escape. Others gird up their loins and advocate nationalizing, or at *least* municipalizing.

I have tried to redirect this optimism, by showing that the evolutionary setting breeds certain pathological results, which call for novel treatments. Entry is a rich subject, with perhaps still more directions than the four I have discussed. Ultimately, it may affect performance more than all the formal rules and procedures. Yet entry is no magic wand, for regulation is a tenacious institution, fundamentally biased against entry and stable against change. Indeed, conventional entry from outside by new sellers may be nearly a dead end, since it goes so thoroughly against the regulatory grain. The other types of entry treat the problem more directly; and they can attract support from important private interests, including the utilities themselves. They offer ways to escape homeostatic border solutions.

At all stages of utility evolution, regulation thus revised may still be inferior to the alternatives, including various forms of public enterprise. Research and trials of new entry should be strictly experimental. If the several entry directions are not effective, we should find out soon, so better treatments can be applied. Much the same is true of public enterprise.

These fundamental experiments with regulation will first have to be designed intellectually, and then carried out legislatively. Neither step will, I predict, be done or even approved by the commissions, even though their tasks would become easier, more interesting, and more effective for the public interest. Our strategy should be, above all, to *anticipate*; to study emergent conditions in traditional utilities and in "new" sectors (cable TV, hospitals), as well as to clarify the sequences of evolution of utilities and regulation. The trade-offs affected by entry and public enterprise—of all sorts—need research. So do their changes during the series of stages.

So far we have embarrassingly vague estimates, at best, and for the older sectors only. Comparative study across sectors, countries, and types of controls is a primary direction for research. Our final objective is to design incentive structures into the regulatory process which will fit the sequence, be neutral toward entry, and give instant carrot-and-stick feeback from performance.

**NOTES TO CHAPTER ONE**

1. American economists, on their part, have quietly let the whole topic fade, hardly mentioning it as a public policy toward business. See Richard E. Caves, "Industrial Organization and Public Policy," a chapter in the survey volume, Nancy Ruggles, ed., *Economics*, Social Science Research Council, Prentice-Hall, 1970; L.W. Weiss, *Case Studies in American Industry*, Wiley, 2nd ed., 1971, last chapter; and F.M. Scherer, *Industrial Market Structure and Economic Performance*, Rand McNally, 1970. By contrast, public ownership is treated extensively, though not analytically, in successive editions of the late Clair Wilcox's Public Policies toward Business, Irwin, 4th ed., 1971. My own little book, *Economic Performance Under Public Enterprise: British Fuel and Power*, Yale University Press, 1965, is virtually the only monograph in the area.

2. See C. Wilcox, *Ibid.*; William A. Robson, *Nationalised Industry and Public Ownership*, Allen and Unwin, 1960; *Annals of Collective Economy*, annual surveys. These survey the old-style public enterprises, and are therefore incomplete, although they are useful beginnings.

3. By "public control" I mean constraints responsive to the general

## 24 Regulation in Further Perspective

public interest, as distinct from special-interest capture of specific programs. The distinction is critical, because programs are often captured and manipulated to benefit narrow, unneedy groups and with inefficient results.

4. I am presently developing these issues in depth in a monograph about policy choices toward market power (*Optimal Industrial Policies*, Columbia University Press, in process). There are hints of them in Mark Green, *The Closed Enterprise System*, Corporate Accountability Research Group, Washington, D.C., 1971. See also P.O. Steiner, *Public Expenditure Budgeting*, Brookings Institution, 1969, and references therein. This is much the same as "program planning and budgeting" (PPB) now common in the federal government but often poorly done.

5. See W.L. Hansen and B.A. Weisbrod, *Benefits, Costs and Finance of Public Higher Education*, Markham, 1969, and W.J. Baumol and W. Bowen, *Performing Arts—The Economic Dilemma*, Twentieth Century Fund, 1966.

6. The President's Commission on Law Enforcement and Administration of Justice, *Crime and Its Impact—An Assessment*, Task Force Report, U.S. Government Printing Office, 1967.

7. See Robson, *op. cit.*; M. Shanks, ed., *Lessons of Public Enterprise*, Jonathan Cape, 1963; W.G. Shepherd, *Economic Performance Under Public Enterprise, op. cit.*

8. W.G. Shepherd, "Alternatives for Public Expenditure," in R.E. Caves and Associates, *Britain's Economic Prospects*, Brookings Institution, 1968.

9. See J. Hughes Chapter 7 in Shanks, *ed. cit.*

10. See, for example, Michael Harrington, "Whatever Happened to Socialism?" *Harper's*, February 1970, pp. 99-105.

11. W.G. Shepherd, "Residence Expansion in British Telephones," *Journal of Industrial Economics*, 1966, pp. 263-74.

12. See W.G. Shepherd and T.G. Gies, eds., *Utility Regulation*, Random House, 1966; A.E. Kahn, *The Economics of Regulation*, Vol. 2, Wiley, 1971.

13. See Caves, *ed. cit.*, Chapter 9 and references there, especially the Sainsbury Committee; Senate Subcommittee on Antitrust and Monopoly, *Report on Administered Prices, Drugs*, 87th Cong., 1st Sess., Report No. 448, U.S. Government Printing Office, 1961; M.J. Peck and F.M. Sherer, *The Weapons Acquisition Process*, Harvard Business School, 1962.

**REFERENCES TO CHAPTER ONE**

J.S. Bain, *Barriers to New Competition*, Cambridge, 1956.

W.M. Capron, ed., *Technological Change in Regulated Industries*, Washington, D.C., 1971.

A.E. Kahn, *The Economics of Regulation*, New York, 1971, 2 vols.

A. Phillips, ed., *Competition and the Regulation of Industry*, Washington, D.C., 1973 (in process).

W.G. Shepherd, "The Elements of Market Structure," *Rev. Econ. Statist.*, Feb. 1972, *54*, 25-37.

———, "Marginal-cost Pricing in American Utilities," *So. Econ. Journ.*, July 1966, *33*, 58-70.

H.M. Trebing, ed., *Performance Under Regulation*, Michigan State University, 1968.

Chapter Two

# Regulatory Reform?

Donald J. Dewey

### Introduction

Some years ago a little noted book appeared with the title *Law: the Science of Inefficiency*. The author was William Seagle. As I recall, the gist of his argument was that however much we may desire legal reform we are not likely to get much of it so long as we stick with the adversary system. He reasoned that half the lawyers have a vested interest in using the inefficiencies of the law to defeat justice. The Constitution may guarantee the defendant the right to a speedy trial; but the last thing desired by a guilty man who can afford bail is a speedy trial. I did not take Seagle's book too seriously at the time, but about a year ago Judge David Bazelon of the United States Court of Appeals went one step further in the *New York Times*.[1] He argued that a more efficient legal system was not even a particularly desirable goal, contending that the court must provide a hearing to people who cannot get it anywhere else in our society. If this involves allowing a litigous paranoid to sue the town council in a federal court because his garbage is not collected on time, so be it.

Both Seagle and Judge Bazelon were adopting extreme positions with which most of us would not concur. Still, I think their observations point to an important truth: reform of the law is so very difficult, precisely because so many people are reasonably happy with the law as it is. My feeling is that this proposition applies especially to regulatory reform. I certainly hope that my remarks will not be taken as a blanket defense of the status quo in regulation. But I also hope that they will clearly convey what I believe: that regulatory reform is not mainly a matter of teaching economics to the public, bringing selfish vested interests to heel, or providing regulatory commissions with more and better staff.

Many years ago it was my good fortune to have as a teacher the late Frank Knight of the University of Chicago, a name known to all economists reading this book. It is probably without significance for the rest, for unhappily, Knight never tried very hard to communicate with any tribe other than his fellow Chicago economists. Knight's idiocyncracies were many; and none was more pronounced than his plain, blunt speech. There was, for example, his proposition, repeated to two generations of students, that economics is really a simple subject. It consisted mainly of telling people things which would be self-evident if they did not have a vested interest in not seeing them.

At the age of nineteen or so, I considered Frank Knight the wisest of men because he had told me so many striking truths that I had never heard before. But along about the time I was 35, when I had learned more of the world, I began to have some doubts about him. The insidious thought started to intrude my mind that perhaps my old teacher was not so much wise as tactless and maybe even mischievous. After all, there are plenty of truths in this world that presumably everybody knows but almost nobody talks about for good and sufficient reasons. Then in my forties my opinion of Knight rose again as a result of my compulsory involvement in the various blow-ups at Columbia University in recent springs, for I then discovered the frightening extent of ignorance and misinformation among my colleagues and students. When so many inhibitions were temporarily cast aside in the spring of 1968, all sorts of strange delusions and paranoia were revealed. It appeared that able graduate students really believed that full professors spent their waking hours maneuvering to become the next department chairman; and that one quiet, mild-mannered scholar was convinced that his salary was being held down by the malice of a dean who may not have even known him by sight. There was also an elderly professor who could not grasp why students were so concerned about the draft law. He pointed out that surely no terrible fate could befall a Columbia College man. At worst he would be given a commission in army intelligence and most likely assigned to Washington.

From these disagreeable experiences in the battles of Morningside Heights I drew a rather obvious conclusion. The only way that we can be sure that a truth is perceived clearly and distinctly is by talking about it—at least every now and then. Coming to our topic, I offer two propositions for your consideration:

1. *Many of the features of the regulatory process extensively discussed by economists and lawyers are not very important.* After all, does it really matter how one computes a fair rate of return on a fair valuation of investment so long as bondholders get their interest and stockholders do not make eye-dazzling capital gains?
2. *Many of the most important features of the regulatory process, for better or worse, are not talked about in public.* I once asked a public service commissioner in an eastern state what his agency did about a utility company that, with the aid of rates approved by it, was earning too high a rate of return on its capital invest-

ment. His answer was, in effect, that the commission did nothing—so long as nobody of political importance complained and so long as the utility company did not have the gall to ask for a rate increase. I suspect that there was a very coherent philosophy of public utility regulation behind this policy. But nobody, to my knowledge, has written it down.

Before going on to defend the two above propositions, I would digress to look briefly at present attitudes toward regulation. Perhaps I should say my remarks apply mainly to the attitudes of economists. (I move in a fairly narrow professional circle.) For our purposes, I think that attitudes toward regulation can be sorted into four boxes. Two of these boxes, as we shall see, are almost (but not quite) empty. To catalogue: we have views which say that regulation is good in theory and good in practice; views that it is good in theory, bad in practice; views that it is bad theory and bad practice. And finally we have views that make it bad in theory, good in practice.

Once upon a time many distinguished economists could be found in the first box—good theory, good practice—with the late Leo Sharfman and John Maurice Clark at their head. Today this box is almost empty. I tentatively put in it the names of James Bonbright, Charles Phillips, and Alfred Kahn. I do so on the suspicion that if they had to choose between living with regulation "as is" and no regulation, they would elect to stick with the status quo.

The second box—good theory, bad practice—is very well populated. It includes all economists who are well disposed to marginal-cost pricing. Incidentally, it also includes the many members of the American Political Science Association who believe that the only one thing wrong with regulation is that it has been captured by its intended victims.

The third box—bad theory, bad practice—is not overcrowded, but it does include the economists (mostly Chicagoans) who have done the most interesting work on regulation in recent years. The Chicago hostility to regulation even as an ideal goes back a long way. Many years ago, Henry Simons wrote

> Unregulated, extra-legal monopolies are tolerable evils; but private monopolies with the blessing of regulation and the support of law are malignant cancers in the system. The conception of regulation as a device for protecting the public against monopoly exploitation is significant, in the real world, mainly as an apology for governmental enforcement of minimum prices and wages at levels higher than monopolies could maintain without the support of law.[2]

In recent years we have had the path-breaking empirical work on the effects of regulation by George Stigler, Paul MacAvoy and their students. My recollection is that in every single case the economic effects of regulation were found to be either non-existent or pernicious.

What of the fourth box—regulation as bad theory but good practice? By this inept choice of words I merely mean to suggest that regulators may be doing praiseworthy work while, at the same time, giving inane or irrelevant reasons for what they do. Incidentally, this possibility is usually reckoned with by students of Frank Knight. He always drummed into us that, for reasons not entirely clear, most people manage to behave more sensibly than they talk. Very possibly there are quite a few people around who believe that regulation is good in practice whatever the avowed theory, but we cannot be sure since nobody speaks up for the view. Therefore, this morning I would like to speak for it myself. Should we assume that I am merely playing the devil's advocate in hopes of heating up the discussion? I really think not. Admittedly it is awfully easy for the professional economist to become facetious whenever the regulation of public utilities is discussed. But this morning I shall do my best to resist this temptation.

I really do believe that Frank Knight was right—most people do manage to act more sensibly than they talk. But as an academic man I also firmly believe that, since talk and action are inseparable, bad theory is likely to produce bad practice. Hence, the bad theory that ostensibly informs the regulation of public utilities is a cause for concern. Perhaps my feeling can best be expressed this way. If regulation in actual operation is, on balance, a good thing, it could be made better if it could be justified by a set of arguments easily understood, communicated, and defended. At the very least, this improvement would make life a lot easier for students in industrial organization courses. For now they must spend an inordinate amount of time learning what is wrong with existing theories of utility regulation.

### A Digression on Taxicabs

Before moving on to a somewhat more systematic defense of my position that regulation is good in practice whatever its theory, I would like to digress and consider what may well be an example of regulation at its very worst. This is the case of the taxicab industry in the city of New York. Here virtually no pretense is made of implementing anything resembling "theory," and most economists regard the results of regulation in this industry as an abomination. I understand that, in some medical circles, it is argued that we can only understand normal biological process by studying pathological deviations. The explanation offered is that such study throws into bold relief causal connections that go unnoticed in a healthy condition. As we shall see, we can regard the results of regulation in Gotham as a variety of extreme regulatory pathology. May we not also assume that if we can find any good in the regulation of taxicabs in New York City, there is certainly something to be said for regulation in the abstract?

Here again I would interject a personal note. Over the past thirty years I have acquired a rather good second-hand acquaintance with high-brow regulatory agencies, most notably the Interstate Commerce Commission, the

Federal Power Commission, and the Federal Communications Commission. My acquaintance with them is second-hand in that it has been gained from gossip and the printed record. I have never played any part in the deliberation of these respected bodies.

I suggest that the distinguishing feature of high-brow regulation is dignity. There is abundant evidence that able lawyers and economists on both sides have worked long and hard on cases; and that commissioners regard themselves as a worthy and important part of the judicial process. But all of my first-hand experience has been with regulation at the state and local level, mainly in New York State. At this low-brow elevation all—or almost all—of the fig leaves are off. A taxicab hearing in my city is likely to have more in common with a pier brawl than it does with the deliberations of the ICC, FPC or FCC. Lest you think that I exaggerate for dramatic effect, I read from the September 15, 1972 issue of the *New York Post:*

> A State Assemblyman and seven other persons were arrested in the Bronx last night after a wild melee involving gypsy cab drivers, policemen and crowds of onlookers. The melee followed a demonstration by the drivers at two intersections . . . Four patrolmen were slightly injured in the disturbance, and a Yellow Cab was smashed and burned by the crowd. The demonstration began at about 7 P.M. Some 100 gypsy cab drivers claiming they had been told earlier in a meeting with Taxi and Limousine Commission officials that their fare meters would have to be removed by October 1, began stalling cabs at two intersections. As traffic in the area began to back up, police moving in to try to clear away the cabs were pelted with rocks and bottles by a crowd of about 200 who had gathered at the scene. At one point, the crowd bolted after a passing yellow cab on Southern Blvd., caught it at a light, pounded in the roof with a hammer, and then set it afire. The driver fled unhurt.

Our first reaction to taxi regulation in New York City is likely to be a mixture of incredulity and outrage. To an economist the most obvious "fact" about New York taxi regulation is the absolutely incredible exploitation of consumers that it makes possible. By the most conservative accounting imaginable, the rate of return on physical capital employed in the industry is at least 100 percent per annum! Five years ago if you wanted to operate a taxicab in New York, your entry cost would have been about $25,000. (Today the entry cost is probably less because of uncertainty about what action the city plans to take against illegally operated ("gypsy") cabs that have appeared on the streets in the last five years.) Such an expenditure would have gotten you a second-hand taxicab worth maybe $1,000; the other $24,000 would have been payment for the medallion or so-called "tin" that allowed you to operate the cab legally. For the record, we are not dealing with an economically trivial industry. In November,

1972 there were about 11,800 legal cabs and 15,000 illegal cabs operating in the city; together they employed over 50,000 drivers and carried more than one million passengers on a business day.

Nor can taxis in New York be described, by any stretch of the imagination, as a luxury good. The elderly, the infirm, the cleaning lady who finishes work at 4 A.M., the mother on welfare who must take four kids with her to the welfare office, have virtually no alternative means of transport. I think it is quite fair to say that each year in my city several hundred muggings, and maybe a few murders, occur because the victims were deprived of the taxicabs which a sensible regulatory policy would have made available. The cause of such staggering exploitation of consumer is, of course, virtually self-evident—restricted entry. The maximum number of cabs that can legally operate in New York is the same now as in 1926. The remedy for such exploitation is equally self-evident—throw the industry open to all competent, financially responsible drivers and let taxi fares be set by competition.

What do New Yorkers get in return for taxicab regulation? The answer has to be, I think, pitifully little. Licensing is a guarantee that the driver has been given a perfunctory screening for character and competence; that the brakes and fare meters have been inspected not too long ago; and that once you get in the cab the driver has to take you where you want to go—unless he wishes to face the risk of a police tribunal before which, of course, the complainant also has to appear.

Do New Yorkers realize that they are being unmercifully exploited? Possibly not. They certainly will not learn about it from the *New York Times* or any public official. Would they be moved to urge free entry into hacking if the facts were explained to them? I doubt it. If the industry were simply thrown open, the many owner-drivers who had put their life savings into a taxicab would be wiped out. And the fledging cab drivers union would be destroyed. New Yorkers are not this callous. If the legal system were without friction, there might be some sentiment for a compensated elimination of taxicab monopoly. But given the way New York courts, legislatures and commissions work, no organized group is prepared to incur the costs necessary to open up the industry through compensation.

So New Yorkers must suffer the status quo of exploitation? Not quite. Taxi fares are set high enough to create franchise value. But for some reason—administrative incompetence, folk wisdom, or pure chance—taxi fares in recent years have not been set high enough to equate our old friends supply and demand. As a result, the poorest parts of the city, which correspond roughly to the high crime areas, simply are not served by legal taxicabs.

Into this vacuum have moved the so-called gypsy cabs. Since gypsies operate in flagrant violation of the law, the police at first tried to suppress them. This led to general community outrage in Harlem and Bedford-Stuyvesant, and soon the gypsies were left alone provided that they did not go outside these areas. Then a year ago drivers of legal cabs went on strike for about a week and the gypsy cabs came swarming off the reservation by the hundreds. Now nobody is quite sure about the territorial division between legal cabs and the gypsies. A gypsy driver will probably be given a summons if he is seen to pick up a fare in central Manhattan. He is still virtually safe in Harlem and Bedford-Stuyvesant. He runs some appreciable risk between 72nd and 125th Streets in Manhattan. As you would expect, the partial success of the gypsies has reduced, but not wholly destroyed, the franchise value of legal (or "yellow") cabs.

Inevitably, a demand has arisen for subjecting the gypsy cabs to some sort of regulation. Naturally, the gypsies would like to be made legitimate and presented with the gift of franchise value. The city's taxicab commission would like to be able to do something about the wretched mechanical condition of the gypsy cabs. As yet, the owners of legal taxicabs oppose extending regulation because they still nurse a faint hope that the police will make the gypsies go away. But I suspect that they will eventually conclude that since you can't lick them, you had better let them join you.

How does an economist react to taxicab regulation? Quite predictably, I think. He denounces all rate regulation except that of the lightest sort. He might, for example, be prepared to accept a rule that requires taxis to stick with whatever rates they elect to set at the beginning of a month for the rest of that month. He might be willing to accept regulation of cab service if he can justify it in terms of externalities. Even a Chicago economist would want the brakes inspected with fair regularity.

Can we now accept that taxicab regulation in New York City is "regulation at its worst"? I think so. If any of you can provide me with a more horrendous example, I shall be glad to use it in my next speech. Most of us will, I think, agree that taxicab reform in New York is mainly a matter of deregulation. But our options to move in this direction are really quite limited. The overnight elimination of entry restrictions is impossible without payment of compensation to the injured. Given law and politics in New York, no compensation is possible; therefore, we must settle for some gradual elimination. As we have seen, this process is now at work, albeit in a very ugly fashion. Police clashes with gypsy drivers have already produced one death and several broken heads, and I fear that more of the same is in the cards before the franchise value of legal cabs is driven close to zero.

It is certainly possible to move in the direction of the elimination of controls on taxicabs. But we might note that cab fares are regulated in virtually every major city of the world and most of the minor ones as well. They are regulated for the very simple reason that we want to be able to get into a cab on a rainy night and have the legal right to be taken to our destination at a legally prescribed fare. Only regulation can confer this power; and if we want it, we have to pay the price. As basic price theory tells us, the price is the creation of franchise value and/or the creation of excess capacity in the industry. Regulation of rates plus entry control insures franchise value. Regulation of rates without entry control insures excess capacity.

It is obvious that most citizens, who know little about franchise value and excess capacity, are prepared to pay a very high price for rainy-night power. What of the all-wise citizen-economist? For myself, I will confess that I am prepared to pay something to have it. In short I accept that there is a legitimate case for rate regulation—even in the case of taxicabs.

I shall go forward to argue that in the case of almost every regulated industry, there is something analogous to rainy-night power in the taxi industry that consumers want. For example, in electrical utilities the analogous power is the right to run an air conditioner all night on the hottest night of the year. And I shall argue that the *raison d'etre* for rate regulation is to be found in these consumer foibles and not in any burning desire to be protected against monopolistic exploitation by avaricious management or victimization by incompetent management.

### Expectations

It is much too glib to say that citizens support regulation to gain rainy-night power in the taxicab industry or hot-weather power in electric utilities. Let us address ourselves to the general question: what do citizens expect from regulation? We might emphasize what this question does not ask. Economists may believe that they know what citizens ought to expect from regulation, but this is another matter. Empirical investigation may reveal that certain labor, management or stockholder interests profit from regulation, but this too is another matter. Again historians may be able to explain why particular industries were brought under regulation in the distant past, but the history of the origins of regulation, while interesting per se to people of antiquarian temperament like myself, is not relevant to the question. It does not tell us why regulation has endured. The question to repeat is: what do citizens expect from regulation? Let us perversely begin with what they do not expect.

> 1. First and foremost they—or should I say we—really do not expect protection from "exploitation" by regulated industries as economists understand this damning term. In the first place, we have no way of telling whether we are being exploited in the sense that the regulated industries are earning more than a fair rate of return on a fair valuation of investment. To say the obvious, as consumers we cannot tell whether an electric or gas rate is "too high" unless we have an expert knowledge of cost functions. Likewise we have no way of knowing whether the price discrimination visited upon us increases or decreases economic welfare.

In the second place, even when we know that we are being exploited in an economic sense—as in the case of New York taxicabs—we may not be much concerned. With the passage of time, monopoly power, however gained in the first place, is made legitimate. It is capitalized into the curve of average cost and transformed into a de facto property right.

As reasonable men and women, we do not consider such a property right to be sacrosanct. (For that matter, we do not believe any property right to deserve complete protection at all times and places.) But we do believe that such capitalized monopoly power—let us call it franchise value—should not be wantonly and decisively destroyed by administrative action. It is one thing for franchise value to be eaten away because the New York police do not now harass gypsy cabs with their former diligence in neighborhoods that legal cabs have mostly abandoned. Some franchise value remains in the taxi industry, and the erosion of this residue promises to be gradual. Moreover, the passing of time has created a counter-vailing set of equities—the established expectations of the unlawful gypsies. These must now also be weighed in the balance. It would be quite another thing for the New York City Council deliberately to wipe out all franchise value in one night by throwing the taxi industry open to all comers.

In criminal law we properly object to the entrapment of criminals except they be of the most odious sort—drug dealers, white slavers, airplane hyjackers or kidnappers. One can argue that in regulated industries franchise value is a sort of entrapment. If it exists, only one inference is possible: the responsible governmental agencies have behaved in a way that brought it into being and hence cannot come into court in any rate case with clean hands. The minimum that we can expect of regulators is that franchise value not be allowed to increase. Our maximum demand is that regulators pursue policies calculated to produce its gradual erosion.

> 2. There is a second result that we most emphatically do not expect from regulation. We do not expect it to serve as a goad to research and development or better management in a regulated industry. Regulatory commissions have neither the resources nor incentives that would allow them to serve this function. More important, we generally want them to serve as a brake on R & D and economically efficient management precisely because progress and efficiency often impose very heavy costs on particular people. Good business practice dictated the elimination of most intercity railroad passenger service at least two decades ago. I, for one, do not object to the policy of the ICC which allowed it to expire slowly. Such a policy provided a grace period to make one's plans and get used to air and bus travel.

So much for what we, as citizens, do not expect from regulation. What then *do* we expect?

Well, first we expect group therapy—a release of tensions and frustrations. Actually I am not playing for a laugh here. When I first went to Duke University many years ago, students ate virtually all their meals in the University dining halls because there were practically no alternatives. A few years later a large private cafeteria opened up in town, and the University's manager of dining halls gave public thanks. He figured the competition would cost him several thousand dollars in income each year but that it would also make his life easier by cutting down on student gripes. Regulated industries tend to be characterized by the absence or near absence of consumer choice—at any rate at certain times and places. This feature breeds an antagonism which is no less real because it is often, by any reasonably objective test, unjustified.

In New York no informed person believes that the recurring power failures of the city are mainly the fault of Consolidated Edison. They can be traced to a faulty rate structure that does not discriminate between peak and off peak demand, and to the ill-conceived obstacles that have been erected to the expansion of generating capacity. Still, a citizen who has been without power for 48 hours in the hottest week of the year is angry; and the object of his rage is Con Ed. The hearings of the Public Service Commission provide one forum in which he can let off steam. There is, of course, no reason why a consumer grievance in a regulated industry cannot be legitimate as well as real. I would only argue that, in the interest of social peace, illegitimate grievances should also be heard. Fortunately, plenty of angry people in this world would rather testify at a public hearing—preferably before a TV camera—than blow up buildings or beat their kids.

Here too I probably generalize on the basis of what I think I have learned in the campus wars of recent springs. What has impressed me most about so-called student rebels is their painful and passionate desire to have somebody just listen to them. As Frank Knight would say, the assumption that the main purpose of talk is action is one of the great heresies of the world. Much talk is simply a release of tension and, so to speak, an end in itself.

Second, we expect regulation to protect us from the kind of sharp commercial practice that is generally impossible in competitive industries. The retailer who sells you a defective radio will take it back and refund your money; otherwise, you will go elsewhere in the future and tell your friends to do likewise. The Penn Central Railroad will never refund a nickel for a breakdown in service unless it is compelled to do so by a Utility Commission.

Third, we expect regulation to mitigate some of the consequences of the bureaucratization that comes with great size. To say the obvious, in any organization mistakes are made, and the larger the organization, the more difficult it is to pinpoint the responsibility for an error. A complaint to a regulatory body is one way that the consumer has of striking back. Not a very effective one, perhaps, but often the best that he has.

Finally, and perhaps most important, we expect that regulation will introduce a little more predictability into our lives. Nine times out of ten when a railroad petitions to abandon service on a branch line, the service should be cut, according to almost any test of economic welfare. Still, using my social welfare function, the welfare loss can be reduced by drawing out the closing process through hearing and review. I will even go out on a limb and offer this proposition for your knives: the principal function of any regulatory agency is to insure a decent respect for the status quo—whatever it happens to be.

To sum up, I put it to you that as citizens we wish the regulatory agency to serve as a forum for group therapy, a better business bureau, a check on bureaucracy, and a brake on economic and social change. Sometimes these goals are compatible with the goal of legislating a competitive rate of return on a correct valuation of assets, or with the goal of a policy of price discrimination endorsed by a majority of economists. But compatibility with these worthy goals cannot always be assumed. At any moment in time regulators must deal with a set of interests and expectations that have been handed to them by industry. For this reason, the early years of regulation in an industry are of crucial importance because they create the constraints which will affect regulation into the distant future.

Have I anything in the way of proof that I have correctly discerned the "true" goals of regulation? While evidence is scattered and inconclusive, I do not believe that it is negligible. For one thing, when economists bring modern econometric techniques to bear on historical data, the oft-told tales about consumer exploitation are revealed mostly to be myths. We all know what George Stigler has done for electrical utilities and Paul MacAvoy for the railroads and natural gas. Most of you will agree, I think, that the same sort of revisionist history can be practiced on every remaining regulated industry with virtually the same results.

If this is true, we are left with two possibilities. The first is that regulation was promoted by interests which hoped to profit from it. This, of course, is the thesis of Gabriel Kolko with regards to railroads. Incidentally, Kolko would better have taken material from electric utilities to illustrate his thesis. For here it is quite clear that many industry figures favored state and federal regulation precisely because they saw it as a protection against local regulation and public ownership. The other possibility is that the citizen advocates of regulation were stupid and/or ill-informed. If so, then regulation should have proved a terrible disappointment to its early supporters. I have found no evidence of their disenchantment in my readings.

Perhaps another possibility should be considered. Is it not possible that idealists bring about regulation in the first place, lose faith in it, but cannot deregulate because the experiment has created too many vested interests? This does not seem to be the case. Otherwise, why do the idealists fail to learn from their experience and keep on looking for more industries to regulate? The correct explanation of the popularity of regulation is, I think, a fairly obvious one. Idealists get much of what they want even though some unattractive vested interests are created in the process.

I have identified what I believe to be the "true" goals of regulation.

They are modest goals and can be pursued without any elaborate superstructure of economic theory or administrative practice. Why then the charade of a five day rate hearing or ten-volume transportation study? Frankly, I do not know; but the need to employ elaborate fictions to justify what one does appears to go rather deep in most humans. The great Frank Knight was content to point out that most people behave more sensibly than they talk. He did not offer a detailed theory of why this is so. Certainly, the use of fictions is by no means confined to regulation; it is even more elaborate in an area of special interest to me—federal antitrust. When I tell people that the best protection against prosecution by the antitrust agencies is to have had a lot of monopoly power for a long time, they think that I am being facetious. I am not being facetious. By the time monopoly rents have been capitalized into common stock prices and labor union contracts, they are nearly immune from government frontal attack. Nevertheless, the legal fiction is that a monopoly rent is not made legal by being capitalized. Whenever a court decides not to disturb capitalized monopoly rent, it cannot simply say that the passing of time makes monopoly legal; it has to produce a long tortuous argument showing either that there really is no monopoly issue, or that it's obviously ineffective remedies are, in fact, effective. In an antitrust case it is usually safe to assume that if a ruling of the court does not seriously alarm labor leaders or stockholders, it will have little economic impact for good or ill.

To take a much more important example of our need for rationalization, we produce all sorts of justifications for the jury system; yet its principal virtue—or any rate the feature that has made for survival—is simply that it limits government and private litigants to enforcing only those laws which have widespread acceptance. Over the centuries, given the prejudices of juries, this has denied what most of us would regard as justice to probably millions of terribly wronged people. But we do not usually talk about this aspect of the jury system.

Suppose for the sake of argument that I have identified the true functions of regulatory process? We can raise again the question: what is to be gained by talking out loud about what everybody takes for granted? One possible benefit has already been suggested. Candor will make easier the teaching of economics. But candor has, I think, other and more important benefits. It may dissuade us citizen-economists from being so contemptuous of the regulatory process and may move us to set lower and more reasonable performance tests. It may stop us from pretending that the only acceptable goal of regulation is to get price equal to marginal cost (where, of course, marginal cost is rising and factor inputs are combined in the most economical way). The payoff to the general public from an honest statement of regulatory purpose would be both tangible and intangible. The obvious, measurable benefit would be a reduction in the cost of administration. If nobody really cares about the real rate of return that the Bell System earns, then why bother with an elaborate investigation, especially since the information will be obsolete for planning purposes next year. As for the intangible benefit to the public from candor about the purposes of regulation, it is simply a more honest form of politics.

### Concluding Remarks

To conclude: Now as always the alternatives to regulation are public ownership and laissez-faire. Yet, if my guesses about the true objects of regulation are reasonably close to the mark, laissez-faire is not a politically feasible alternative in this country. For—and I apologize for repeating myself—the demand for regulation is ultimately rooted in the absence of consumer choice and the frustrations that result. These frustrations got us regulation in the first place; the fact that we almost never move to deregulate strongly suggest that regulation does deliver much of whatever citizens expect of it.

Public ownership is now, I believe, a politically acceptable alternative in most regulated industries, even though there may be no convincing economic case to be made for it. What happens to the functions previously exercised by a regulatory agency when the industry is transferred to public ownership? If one has complete faith in the wisdom and fairness of the managers of the state enterprise, the very *raison d'etre* of regulation disappears. In the absence of such total faith, the regulatory functions must be assumed by elected officials—a worthy but erratic group. Or they must be vested in some sort of appeals tribunal. Indeed, it is precisely the powers that we would not entrust to the managers of a "natural" monopoly under public ownership that we give to regulators when the industry is privately owned.

I fear that in this chapter I have seemed to downgrade the importance of the whole regulatory process; seemed to have sneered at the efforts of conscientious economists and lawyers who search everyday for a fair rate of return on a fair valuation of investment; and seemed to imply that a degree in psychiatric social work is the best preparation for an appointment to a regulatory commission. Please accept that I do not wish to leave this impression behind. The late Frank Knight also drilled into his students that economics is not nearly as important as most people believe; and that, to use a popular modern term, most of the really important problems of this world involve conflict-resolution where good economic theory is of only limited usefulness.

The citizen who believes that he has been unfairly dealt with by Consolidated Edison may be psychotic or merely misinformed, but it is not good politics to let his grievance fester or be subjectively transformed into a grievance against somebody else—most probably the members of his local school board. Political democracy requires safety valves as well as pistons. The interminable rate hearing is one such safety valve and so is to be accounted a beneficient institution. Let me assure you that I do not sneer at it.

I fear that some readers will have been disappointed in my remarks, if only because I have said nothing about the nuts and bolts problems of regulatory reform. In all honesty I cannot get excited about them. The technical reforms that you want depend mainly upon what changes in regulatory goals you want, and here my conservatism verges on black reaction. With regard to the big directional changes in regulation, economists are of two minds. One says that the only meaningful regulatory reform is the elimination of regulation. I cannot get excited about this goal, because I am sure that the citizenry will not buy it, and I am not sure that they should buy it.

Economists of the second persuasion say that regulation should be made more effective. In their view the essence of effective regulation is to keep a regulated industry balanced precariously on some fair rate of return. We all know what happens when, for some reason, the regulators miscalculate and set the rate of return too low. In New York City the monument to this kind of miscalculation in the area of rent control is several hundred abandoned apartment buildings—they just were not worth maintaining at the maximum legal rents. New York is the only city in the country still operating under the wartime system of rent control that was abandoned everywhere else by 1954. Why this is so, is a long and sad story.

I find utility regulaticn tolerable precisely because it is usually inefficient and hence provides a margin of safety for the regulators. Far better to get your service from a fat subsidiary of Bell Telephone under casual state regulation than from a railroad teetering on the edge of bankruptcy under effective federal regulation. No doubt there are many nuts and bolts reforms on which we could all agree such as air conditioned hearing rooms or faster publication of rulings. I suspect that they would not serve to generate anything in the way of either a lively or rewarding discussion.

**NOTES TO CHAPTER TWO**

1. David L. Bazelon, "A Probing Role for the Courts," *New York Times*, August 21, 1971.
2. Henry Simons, *Economic Policy for a Free Society* Chicago, 1948, p. 86.

Chapter Three

# A Critique of Regulatory Accommodation to Change

Harry M. Trebing

**Introduction**

The question of regulation's ability to accommodate change, while at the same time imposing constraints that protect the public interest, is challenging, frustrating and far from resolved. Basically, what is involved is the confrontation between broad propulsive forces for change, on the one hand, and the adaptability or resiliency of the institutional system of supply on the other. This conflict brings into play new technology, new patterns of demand, potential entrants, and the responses of the established public utilities, common carriers, and regulatory agencies.*

Much of the current discontent with regulation has focused implicitly or explicitly on this capacity to accommodate change. The well-known allegations regarding regulation's hostility toward new entrants: its desire to maintain the status quo, and its preoccupation with *ex post* criteria for fixing prices and earnings, are frequently cited as major failures of the existing commission system.

The relevant alternatives for public policy, however, are not as simple as the critics of regulation would lead one to believe. In the fields of electricity, gas and communications, the choice is not between a market structure that is inherently competitive and continued reliance on an ineffectual, cumbersome bureaucratic process. Indeed, there is an imposing array of factors which serve to indicate that highly imperfect market structures can be expected to continue into the future and that some form of social intervention will be necessary. First, concentration will remain high because decreasing costs, relative to the size of the market, prevail in major segments of energy and communications supply. Second, the high threshold investment characteristic of those industries

---

*The author gratefully acknowledges the valuable assistance obtained in various conversations with David S. Schwartz.

which must maintain a broad network to serve a widespread market of small users constitutes a significant barrier to entry. Third, there is a high degree of interdependence in corporate decision making because of the variety of institutional and technical arrangements which tie the operations of firms together through grids, interconnected systems, division of revenues, toll settlements, power pools and interchange agreements. Fourth, technical conditions associated with the provision of service limit the number of suppliers at particular stages or phases of the operation, thereby creating potentially monopolistic conditions. Fifth, consumer demands for utility services as necessities are vulnerable to manipulation and discriminatory pricing by highly concentrated industries. Sixth, there are important externalities associated with the production and consumption of such services. And seventh, there are equity and fairness considerations involved in the distribution of basic utility services.

Accordingly, a more realistic choice involves either deregulation, which implies reliance on highly imperfect market structures constrained (or possibly maintained) by gradually relaxed and largely ineffective controls, or an effort to improve the process of social control in a fashion that enhances industry performance consistent with public requirements. For all except the most doctrinaire critics of regulation, the latter course of action deserves investigation. An examination of the ability of the commission system to accommodate change, together with an exploration of opportunities for improvement, is central to such an inquiry.

### Conflicting Pressures and Change under Regulation

Change taking place in a regulatory setting is characterized by a traditional division of responsibilities. To management goes the authority to initiate service offerings, establish new prices and tariffs, formulate investment and financing programs, and incur expenses. To regulation goes the authority to review such actions, suspend rates and tariff changes for determinate periods pending further inquiry, and disallow expenses. Within these limits, the exercise of managerial prerogatives permits the enterprise to pursue a variety of objectives and strategies. The theory of the firm under regulatory constraints provides some insight into corporate behavior and possible inducements for change. But a parallel theory of regulatory behavior is far from complete and inferences can only be pieced together from an examination of regulatory techniques and practices. Clearly, both theories are needed to permit a rigorous analysis of regulatory accommodation to change.

By the same token, there is very little empirical information available to define what constitutes optimal performance in the regulated industries. This makes it difficult to measure the degree to which regulatory success or failure in accommodating change accounts for deviations from an optimal path.

These drawbacks, however, do not preclude a consideration of regulatory accommodation which can be achieved by examining individual case studies in which commissions have sought to come to grips with changes of major proportions. Such case studies should reveal infirmities, weaknesses, possible strengths, and ultimately provide a basis for generalizations about the process and for determining inherent barriers to effective accommodation to change as well as a means for achieving improvements.

**Three Case Studies**

The case studies to be discussed describe three major changes, each different in form but each calling for decisive regulatory action. The first deals with the reaction of the Federal Communications Commission to new technology in common carrier communications; the second deals with the reaction of the Federal Power Commission to the natural gas shortage; the third deals with the reaction of the Postal Rate Commission to the challenge of regulating a newly constituted government corporation.

1. **New Technology in Communications.** The market structure of the domestic common carrier communications industry remained remarkably stable from 1913 through the 1950s. The American Telephone & Telegraph Company's dominant position, as well as its overwhelming share of the market, stood unchallenged. The independent telephone companies and Western Union existed largely at the sufferance of the Bell System. More important, Bell administered the rate of technological advance through its vertical affiliate, Western Electric, and its research arm, Bell Laboratories. For the most part, commissions complemented this condition through the enforcement of tariff restrictions on foreign attachments and interconnection, and by their indifference toward the certification of new entrants, although it must be admitted that challenging Bell with existing technology would have been foolhardy at best.

Government sponsored research during World War II and the years immediately thereafter seriously weakened Bell's control over new technology.[1] Satellite, microwave and laser technology gave promise of reducing transmission costs. Similarly, new developments in terminal hardware gave promise of greater audio-video-data flexibility and new usage patterns.

These changes, in turn, were accompanied by a desire on the part of potential consumers and suppliers to utilize the new technology in a fashion and at a rate other than that prescribed by AT&T. The problem came to a head when private parties sought to develop microwave transmission and were challenged by Bell in their efforts to secure access to the radio frequency spectrum. The issue was joined in the "Above 890" case, which the FCC decided in 1959 by opening that portion of the frequency spectrum above 890 megacycles to private entry.[2] This historic decision constituted a significant step in the direction of relaxed entry; and although it was almost a decade before the next major entry cases were decided, it was clear that the FCC would not foreclose entry simply to maintain the position of an established carrier.

In the Carterfone decision (1968) and the MCI decision (1969)[3] the FCC reiterated its stand against what it perceived to be artificial barriers to entry. The Carterfone decision served to declare artificial foreign attachment restrictions unlawful. The MCI decision authorized Microwave Communications, Inc., to provide specialized carrier service on a limited point-to-point basis for private-line customers. This decision was followed in 1971 by a general policy statement endorsing free entry by specialized carriers.[4] The Domestic Satellite decision (1972)[5] appeared to reiterate this policy when the Commission declared its receptiveness to liberalized entry in satellite as well as terrestrial communications.[6]

In effect, when confronted with new technology and new demands, the FCC opted for liberalized entry, greater freedom of consumer choice and a pluralistic market structure and rejected the arguments based on natural monopoly, systemic integrity and a chosen-instrument policy. There is recent evidence that a similar policy may be emerging among state commissions which have traditionally been far less charitable toward such departures from orthodoxy.[7]

Undoubtedly, advocates of competition will be pleased with the FCC's policy of flexibility as a means of accommodating change, yet there are serious questions whether such relaxations alone are sufficient to accommodate new technology. To be successful, new technology must be incorporated into service offerings with some portion of the net gain ultimately passed forward to the consumer. In response to the "Above 890" decision, AT&T introduced a complex series of new tariff offerings, designed to foreclose prospective competition in the private-line markets. When its traditional value-of-service criteria were seriously questioned as a viable constraint on cross-subsidization, it also introduced long-run incremental cost (LRIC) as a basis for a "burden test" which would allegedly curb cross-subsidization between competitive and monopoly markets. The alternative test, i.e., fully distributed costs, was regarded with considerable apprehension by Bell because of the greater limitations that it would place on managerial discretion in reacting to threats of competitive diversion.

There appears to be no end to the pricing variants which Bell has been able to develop; and, indeed, much of the time of the FCC has been devoted to grappling with these tariffs on a case-by-case basis. The initial Telpak tariff was only one example of a series of new proposals that included WATS, WADS, Telpak-sharing restrictions, the Series 11,000 tariffs, DUV (data under voice) and more recently "Hi-Lo" density rates.[8] In the future it is also likely that network access pricing and new bulk rate tariffs will be proposed. The former would "unbundle" tariffs into a charge for access and usage and a charge for terminal equipment.

Whether the great mass of consumers has benefitted from such changes can be debated. Departures from system-wide averaging are certain to become a permanent feature for large volume users of private line circuits. Also, rates for some facilities, such as terminal equipment, may gravitate toward costs.

Yet, have such changes benefitted the users of the monopolistic message toll telephone service? The fact remains that Bell proposed to raise the general level of message toll telephone rates by two percent in Docket No. 19129, while at the same time arguing that private line charges were fully compensatory and need not be increased. Further, Bell sought to reduce monthly rates on series 200 data sets by 35 percent in a market that was argued to be competitive.[9]

The FCC has endeavored to establish pricing guidelines for individual service offerings. However, after lengthy hearings in Docket No. 16258 and further hearings in Docket No. 18128, the Commission seems unable to arrive at a clear-cut, all-pervasive solution in the contest between LRIC and FDC. Indeed, the debate now seems to have spread to the state level.

In the absence of generally acceptable pricing guidelines, it is not unexpected that the FCC would adopt a market-shares policy to prevent unwarranted exercise of corporate power and cross-subsidization by common carriers. The result has been an effort to compartmentalize monopoly and supposedly competitive markets by limiting or circumscribing the actions of carriers in the latter. This has taken place principally in CATV and data processing services.[10]

The results of such a policy cannot be readily discerned at the present time. There may be significant social costs in the form of the inefficient use of resources, but there is not sufficient information available about system optimization or the existence of redundant plant to make a sophisticated judgment. Similarly, there is the possibility that such a market-structure policy will be eroded or circumvented by holding company diversification in the case of non-Bell companies. Finally, there is the prospect that foreclosure of carriers from markets of rapid potential growth will increase the cost of capital and therefore raise rates to consumers of the monopoly services. Again, the validity of these arguments remains to be assessed—both in theory and in quantitative terms.

On balance, the FCC has not sought to stifle technology in order to maintain the status quo. Yet the FCC experience has shown that relaxation of entry restrictions *per se* is no assurance of smooth, orderly accommodation to change. Four observations can be made:

First, the reaction of established firms must be anticipated and suitable pricing guidelines developed to minimize both potential discrimination and cross-subsidization. Indeed, a major consequence of liberalized entry may be the promotion of more refined price discrimination and non-price rivalry rather than the attainment of the price-cost-output equilibria normally associated with workable competition.

Second, there is no assurance that the rivalry between common and specialized carriers, or between carriers and interconnect companies, will approximate workable competition. On the contrary, there is considerable evidence that an oligopolistic interdependence of firms and the need to come to terms on issues like interconnection may compel tacit collusion and a new round of efforts to foreclose further entry. Nevertheless, the Carterfone and MCI decisions have created new dimensions of rivalry in markets such as terminal equipment and software, which theoretically can be used to stimulate innovation and change.

Third, there seems to be an inability on the part of the parties involved to formulate the relevant conceptual issues and resolve them in an expeditious fashion that is acceptable to all participants. This is amply demonstrated by the ten-year lag in formulating pricing guidelines and the four-year lag in resolving interconnection issues associated with Carterfone. The interconnection problem indicates another phenomenon, namely, recourse to long-term studies and the creation of inter-agency committees as a means of handling the problem.[11]

Fourth, the chronic data-information gap continues to beset FCC regulation on these pricing and market structure issues.

**2. Natural Gas Shortage.** The natural gas market has changed from one in which supplies were in abundance to one in which current stocks are in short supply. The natural gas shortage has resulted in severe service disruptions for the transmission pipelines and distribution companies. Many pipelines are in curtailment, and distribution companies are restricting sales to new customers. Further, uncertainty regarding future supplies has apparently convinced some pipelines that continued growth requires diversification into non-regulated activites. State commissions have played a limited role as far as the shortage is concerned, and attention has focused primarily on the actions of the Federal Power Commission. Again, accommodation to change is the central theme.

Critics allege that the FPC has held price below the equilibrium that would have prevailed in the marketplace; hence, demand exceeds supply at the administered price level and gas has become a misallocated resource in short supply.[12] The appropriate solution, critics argue, is to permit market forces to set prices at the wellhead and thereby ration use, promote conservation, increase reserves, and assure abundant supplies. Interestingly, this simplistic solution appears to have been accepted by the FPC itself. Since early 1969, the Commission has followed a program designed to escalate field prices in order to expand supplies.

Over time, FPC policies with respect to the regulation of independent gas producers provide a classic illustration of vacillation and procrastination in the face of a major national problem. Between 1946 and 1954,[13] the agency wrestled with the question of jurisdiction over producers. Between 1954 and 1965,[14] it struggled to establish an appropriate ratemaking method to apply to the field price of gas. Between 1965 and 1968, it sought to refine and apply the area pricing concept, which it had adopted, to major producing fields.[15] Between 1969 and the present time, the FPC has endeavored to qualify and, in effect, dismantle its previous regulatory approach to field prices on the grounds that it was no longer appropriate in the face of a gas shortage.

Commission-endorsed price escalation has taken the form of modifications in and departures from the established policy of fixing ceiling prices by major gas producing areas. The following decisions serve to illustrate this change in policy. In Dockets No. R-389 and R-389A, the FPC indicated its willingness to consider a demonstration by independent producers that special circumstances justified a higher price than that prevailing under the area ceiling rates in order to secure new gas sales for interstate markets. In Order No. 428 it exempted the interstate sales of 4,600 small independent producers from area price ceilings. In Order No. 431 it authorized short-term emergency contracts for rates in excess of area ceilings upon a showing by a pipeline that there was a threat of curtailed usage. In Docket No. R-441 it permitted "optional pricing," giving the pipeline the option of proceeding under area rates or of direct negotiation with a gas producer. While the negotiated contract would be subject to FPC review, it is clear that the conditions imposed are far from stringent.[16]

As a further inducement to expand gas supplies, the FPC allowed pipelines to make interest-free loans to gas producers in the form of advance payments. Advance payments for production and exploration would remain in the rate base until drawn down by subsequent deliveries, thereby minimizing the financial risk borne by the pipeline. The Commission also has under consideration a proposal for an exploration program sponsored by a distribution company that would, in effect, drastically alter the market structure of the industry. It would allow distribution companies to enter into exploration, development and production, and then utilize the interstate pipelines simply to transport these new discoveries.

The ultimate test, of course, is whether these policies have significantly increased the supply of gas during the period 1969 through 1972. The best available measure to answer this question is the findings-to-production ratio. This contrasts annual *additions* to reserves to annual net production. For the early period (1946-1954) in which the FPC was uncertain as to jurisdiction, the average annual ratio was 2.18; for the next period (1954-1965) the average annual ratio was 1.54; for the post-Permian period (1965-1968) the ratio was 1.03. The lowest ratio recorded between 1946 and 1967 was 1.0. In 1968 the ratio dropped sharply to 0.6, but since the shift in FPC policy, the F/P ratio has remained distressingly low: 1969: 0.4; 1970: 0.5; 1971: 0.4; and 1972: 0.4.[17]

It can, of course, be argued that a four-year period is insufficient to test the change in FPC regulatory policy. A more plausible explanation of the low F/P ratio is that the Commission has disregarded rudimentary economic logic by concentrating its efforts on allowing prices to escalate on a piecemeal basis. It is irrational to believe that a natural gas producer will commit large reserves of gas to interstate commerce at a fixed price as long as he anticipates that the price will continue to increase over time.[18] On April 10, 1973, Chairman Nassikas effectively extended the time horizon for this expectation by arguing that Congress should remove "FPC price control . . . for contract commitments to the interstate market of gas from new discoveries, dedications and wells . . . ,"[19]

During this period of price escalation there is very little evidence that the FPC considered in a sophisticated fashion either the market structure of the gas industry or the total energy picture.

The Commission has appeared to be indifferent to matters either of economic concentration among producers or of corporate power. It seems to have implicitly accepted the hypothesis that the pipeline oligopsony of the immediate postwar period had evolved into a market structure in which arm's-length bidding between pipelines and producers for new gas was a reasonable proxy for competition. One suspects that this belief has been corroborated insofar as the Commission is concerned by the relatively low over-all or aggregate concentration ratios for all gas sales in interstate commerce.[20]

The number of unknowns, however, is simply too great to justify accepting this hypothesis without further research. The biggest problem is the lack of data pertaining to reserves. As Hughes and Francis note: "Almost two decades after the FPC was given the authority to regulate producers, it is still in a state of ignorance about the particulars of the industry's reserves data."[21] The only public information available on proved reserves is supplied by industry. There is no information publicly available on total uncommitted reserves. Further, there is no information available on uncommitted reserves by source of ownership or control, by major producing area, or by major producing field.

In addition, aggregate concentration ratios for total gas sales in interstate commerce can be misleading. It is more important to focus on the major producing area or major producing field as the relevant market for judging the presence or absence of competitive bargaining. The FPC does have data on gas sales by individual producers once a contract is consummated; but this can only be contrasted with data for aggregate sales already committed, or flowing, from the area. What is needed are data which reflect concentration in terms of new sales, giving weight to currently available supplies, augmented by concentration data on uncommitted reserves by producing area.

Of course, concentration ratios alone are insufficient. Collective arrangements among producers for the exploration of new gas, especially in offshore areas, as well as similar arrangements pertaining to the sale of this gas are of considerable importance. These institutional phenomena must be considered together with proper concentration data to assess corporate power and collusive action.

There are other dimensions of market structure which have received little formal attention in Commission decisions. For example, it is difficult to discern what weight has been given to the potential for extortion and exercise of corporate power inherent in bilateral oligopoly where the position of the independent producers is greatly enhanced by the scramble among pipelines to commit new reserves to interstate commerce. Further, the countervailing bargaining power anticipated from both distribution companies and from pipelines will be considerably diminished when these pipeline and distribution companies purchase gas for ultimate sale in markets where demand is growing rapidly and at the same time becoming more price inelastic due to the superiority of the fuel in meeting ecological standards.[22]

Also, the FPC seems to have great confidence in interenergy rivalry as a means of constraining abusive practices. This confidence, however, may be misplaced since interenergy rivalry, like interindustry rivalry, is a very poor proxy for intraindustry competition in assuring that firms will adopt the most efficient scale of production and that prices in the long run will equal costs plus a normal rate of profit. In addition, the Commission does not appear to have given sufficient analytical attention to the impact of growing concentration in the energy field resulting from the growth of energy companies. These companies have significant holdings in oil, natural gas and coal reserves, and the consequences of this form of concentration for interenergy rivalry as a constraint on price increases are obvious.

Insofar as the total energy picture is concerned, there is little doubt that the Commission is aware of the place of gas in a larger setting. At various times the FPC has authorized more Canadian imports, supported the Alaska pipeline, and commented on import quotas.[23] Indeed, the suggestion has even been made that the FPC be reconstituted as a Federal Energy Commission.

Unfortunately, the FPC has not taken more than the most rudimentary steps in the direction of placing gas within a national energy context. The persistent data-information gap still prevails for other forms of energy as well as gas. For example, the data deficiencies on gas production costs extend to the cost of producing alternative new forms of energy, such as the gasification of coal, through pilot projects of sufficient size to give an adequate indication of all potential economies of scale.

Nevertheless, the FPC does deserve credit for initiating the National Gas Survey in 1971. Many of the topics designated for coverage are relevant to the gas shortage.[24] However, as is too often the case, the results will not be available until years after the FPC has embarked on its policy of ceiling price escalation. It is too early to speculate on the quality of the Survey; as a joint industry-government endeavor it may suffer from those characteristics common to all committee efforts.

In summary, it appears that the FPC experience provides three important insights into the process of regulatory accommodation to change:

First, the effective handling of a major national problem such as the gas shortage requires a capacity for long-term planning and an over-all perspective. Such planning involves more than a simple enumeration of selected factors or an endorsement of new sources of supply. It requires an independent data base, a recognition of the interrelationship between strategic variables, and an appreciation of industry structure. It is doubtful that the Commission came close to satisfying these conditions, either in the period 1969-1972, or in most of the earlier years.[25]

Second, a period of change comparable to 1969-1972 requires that the regulatory agency serve as a custodian of the public interest in the face of conflicting signals. At present there is a danger of succumbing to a gas shortage psychosis. This fear could rebound to the benefit of gas suppliers who are able to turn the situation into an apologetic for raising prices as a means of achieving conservation. It is certainly open to debate whether the FPC has fulfilled its custodial role by screening these claims of a gas-energy crisis to determine their validity. In fact, on the basis of present information, the Commission cannot give a definitive answer to the question raised by consumer advocates: is the shortage real, in the sense of resource exhaustion, or is it contrived, in the sense that exploration and reserves are being withheld pending higher prices?

Third, a period of change typically calls for regulatory creativity and experimentation. There is little evidence that the FPC pushed the frontiers of regulatory knowledge during 1969-1972. It did little, for example, to develop new ratemaking techniques to replace the area pricing concept. Instead, it relied on gradual price escalation in highly imperfect markets, without price-cost criteria sufficient to monitor the existence of excessive economic rents. Similarly, it did little to explore institutional alternatives to open up new gas reserves—especially on public lands. Yet it is not unreasonable for the Congress and the public to expect new thoughts from the agency in these areas.

**3. Regulating Postal Rates.** The third case study of accommodation to change focuses on the role of regulation during the first phase of the conversion of the Postal Service from an old-line government department to a semi-autonomous independent government enterprise.

Criticism of the Post Office Department had been mounting in the 1960s, culminating in the report of the Kappel Commission.[26] Convinced that improvement lay in the direction of greater autonomy and freedom from political encumbrances, Congress created the United States Postal Service in 1970.[27] At the same time, it established the Postal Rate Commission, a regulatory agency with ratemaking responsibility. Almost immediately, the USPS moved to increase rates as the first step in a ten-year program to make the service financially self-sustaining. The resulting case (Docket No. R71-1) marked the first adjudicatory proceeding involving postal rates to come before an independent commission.

The USPS had relatively little experience in formal ratemaking proceedings, and the PRC had no legacy of past decisions and no inherited expertise in postal ratemaking to draw upon. In a sense the slate was clean—for better or for worse.

Any significant increase in postal rates was certain to elicit a strong reaction from those users of the mails who had enjoyed preferential status for many years as well as from those who had enjoyed low rates for bulk mailings.

As a consequence, the USPS felt that it had to consider possible effects on its revenues stemming from a diversion of business to other forms of communications and transport as well as to other carriers. Legal monopoly insulated much of the first-class service from direct competition; but second, third and fourth-class mail service was apparently perceived by the USPS as susceptible to varying degrees of diversion. Indeed, more than 50 percent of the parcel market had already been lost to United Parcel Service.

The pricing problems confronting the USPS were further complicated by the fact that the service had begun a massive construction program to establish a new nation-wide bulk mail handling network. Any significant diversion of those classes of mail that would utilize this facility would clearly jeopardize both the success of the project and the Postal Service's objective of financial self-sufficiency.

Against this background USPS developed its case, covering three areas: (1) total revenue requirements; (2) the allocation of these requirements to types of customers and classes of mail; and (3) specific price changes.

Major attention focused on the distribution of aggregate revenue requirements to different types of customers and different classes of mail. The USPS proposed a three-part procedure for accomplishing this objective. First, attributable costs were to be estimated. This category included all costs, both variable and fixed, that could be directly imputed or traced to a particular class of service. Second, institutional costs would be calculated; these were essentially the residual overhead or common costs which represented the difference between total costs and the sum of all attributable costs. Third, institutional costs would be allocated to various classes of service on the basis of demand criteria and Congressional guidelines.

Attributable costs were particularly important since they were to serve as the basis for establishing the minimum revenue requirements by class of service. The concept and measurement of attributable costs, as presented by USPS, was somewhat unique. Attributable costs were designated as short-run incremental costs. This definition stemmed from the fact that they were composed primarily of directly assignable costs that varied with volume on a year-to-year basis. To these costs were added any directly assignable fixed costs. In total, attributable costs accounted for approximately 50 percent of all postal system costs on an annual basis.

The USPS justified this concept of attributable costs on the grounds that: (1) short-run costs reflect the labor-intensive character of postal costs, and therefore provide a better means of monitoring potential imbalances in revenues and expenses; (2) the theoretical and applied difficulties of measuring long-run incremental costs are great, while the measurement of short-run attributable costs is more accurate; and (3) short-run costs facilitate a policy of maximizing the contribution to institutional costs from non-monopoly services in order to minimize the burden of institutional costs on monopoly services.

As might be expected, the attributable cost concept was vigorously contested by intervenors and the Litigation Staff of the PRC. Some witnesses argued that a much higher proportion of costs could have been assigned to the attributable category had the USPS used appropriate quantitative techniques. Others argued that fully distributed cost studies were preferable on the grounds that economies of scale were negligible. Still others argued that LRIC was far preferable to SRIC in decisions involving the expansion of capacity. Finally, various witnesses debated the relevance, if any, of equating the USPS costing concepts with the economists' definition of short- and long-run costs.

At the conclusion of the proceeding, two major imponderables confronted the Commission. The first was whether the basic set of welfare conditions necessary for the employment of the Postal Service's incremental costing proposal had been satisfied. The second was the need to rely on data which had been generated through concepts and techniques that were of dubious theoretical or applied validity.

Incremental costing could conceivably benefit consumers if: (1) one or more services have an elastic demand function in the face of a proposed rate change; (2) the services share significant costs in common; and (3) there are economies of scale in the area of common costs.[28] In such a setting, it is possible that reduced rates in elastic markets could promote usage and thereby lower unit costs for all services as well as absorb a portion of overhead or institutional costs that would otherwise have to be borne by inelastic markets.

There are certain obvious common costs in providing postal service, but no hard empirical evidence was introduced into the record to show that economies of scale exist. On the contrary, independent econometric studies strongly suggested that constant returns to scale exist and decreasing returns to scale were quite probable.[29] If constant returns did prevail, then the difference between full cost and incremental cost would become more a matter of prescribing acceptable accounting standards than a debate over the merits and faults of marginal and average cost pricing.

There was a similar lack of conclusive evidence that any major class of mail was characterized by an elastic demand function. Existing studies made use of historical data and generally indicated that demand was very inelastic. The USPS argued that it was more important to consider "prospective" elasticities (i.e., elasticities expected to prevail at future prices). Yet no one produced such estimates, undoubtedly because of the difficulty of forecasting cross-elasticities. Mathematica did attempt to forecast elasticity values for a range of price increases for selected postal services and found demand to be highly inelastic.[30]

To the degree that these conditions were not satisfied, the USPS' SRIC ratemaking proposal became nothing more than an *ad hoc*, pragmatic solution justified solely on the grounds of expedience.

The uncertainties surrounding these underlying assumptions also aggravated the overall data problem, for the submissions of the Postal Service constituted the only general source of data. The PRC was faced, therefore, with

## A Critique of Regulatory Accommodation to Change 53

a series of dilemmas. It resolved the difficulties by neither accepting nor rejecting the USPS' ratemaking principles. Instead, it proceeded to prescribe a rate structure and promulgate a rulemaking proceeding to further explore the problem of appropriate pricing principles.[31] This rulemaking subsequently had to share the attention of the agency with the general reclassification case (*Postal Classification, 1973,* Docket No. MC73-1), which was required by the Postal Reorganization Act. As a practical matter, this meant that any decision regarding pricing principles would be deferred for an indefinite period.

Paralleling the debate over ratemaking principles and establishing prices is the much broader question of the performance of the Postal Service. After all, the major reason for creating the Postal Service was to improve the performance record of the old Post Office Department. This issue was raised, but not resolved, in Docket No. R71-1. Recent activity by Congressional committees indicates that there is no prospect that the topic will become dormant.

The USPS has moved to establish quality of service standards in the form of National Service Goals.[32] By early 1973, formal goals had only been established for air mail and local first-class mail; however, it was considered likely that delivery targets would eventually be extended to other classes of mail. The National Service Index serves to measure the attainment of these goals as well as the performance of the postal system. The NSI provides data from 1968 to date covering handling time or "average days to delivery" for selected types of mail.[33] In addition to NSI, the Postal Service calculates a variety of productivity ratios and keeps records on matters such as personnel turnover and maintains an elaborate workload reporting system.

The long-term performance record of the postal system gives cause for concern. Productivity per employee increased at an average annual rate of 2.1 percent over the period 1908-1931. For the period 1908 to 1953, inclusive, it increased at an average annual rate of 1.8 percent. For the period 1953-1969, the average annual increase in productivity was 0.2 percent.[34] It is particularly distressing that the years since 1953 have seen the introduction of new mail processing machines and mechanized handling facilities without a discernible rate of growth in employee productivity. Further, the NSI's measure of elapsed days to delivery remained static for various types of mail between FY 1970 and FY 1971.[35] USPS has, on the other hand, argued that productivity for clerks and mail handlers increased 3.3 percent in terms of pieces of mail per workhour and increased 1.5 percent for deliveries per workhour for city delivery carriers between FY 1970 and FY 1971.[36]

On balance, the performance record of USPS remains depressing and the data-information base leaves a number of important questions unresolved. For example, the productivity ratios cited by USPS are partial productivity measures. Would an on-going series of total factor productivity measures, giving weight to capital as an input, yield different results? Also, existing productivity measures fail to reflect customer-performed services (such as presorting) as inputs, but the resultant mail volume is included in output. This distortion suggests that current productivity measures may tend to overstate the actual rate of productivity gain.

Unfortunately, as of early 1973, the PRC had done nothing to require that the USPS file the necessary information to develop a full set of independent productivity and performance measures. In the absence of such data it will be difficult, if not impossible, for the regulatory agency to undertake the sophisticated quantitative analysis necessary to explain performance levels in terms of relevant causal factors. It will also be difficult for the PRC to evaluate the chronic argument that the Postal Service is in a state of transition and that various short-term compromises in ratemaking will have to be tolerated in order to attain long-run improvements in efficiency. As a practical matter, the agency will be left with the difficult decision of granting successive rate increases without commensurate independent information on changes in the level of performance.

The PRC experience leads to the following observations on regulatory accommodation to change:

First, the data-information gap seems to be endemic to all regulation, whether the regulated enterprise is private or publicly owned. Data and information sources are jealously guarded by the regulated firm, and neither public nor private enterprise is particularly solicitous of regulation's information needs.[37] Further, Docket No. R71-1 indicates how a regulated enterprise can structure the character of the available data and its inherent validity by the ratemaking principles or concepts that it chooses to employ. Effective regulation and planning require that this type of situation be avoided.

Second, major problems and ambiguities pertaining to ratemaking principles and theories have a way of being carried forward to future cases or actions without being resolved.[38] Confronted by conflicting testimony, agencies such as the PRC and the FCC have a propensity to defer reaching conclusions. There seems to be an abiding faith that future decisions will be able to resolve what current and past decisions could not.

Third, it is reasonable to assume that the PRC should serve as a public-interest ombudsman *vis-à-vis* the Postal Service. This means that the regulatory agency should maintain an independent series of performance measures and specify service standards.[39] In the absence of service standards, the consumer has incomplete knowledge upon which to base decisions. In the absence of performance data, the regulatory body has no independent basis for monitoring change.

Fourth, the question of the legitimacy of the postal monopoly in letter mail and continued subsidization in other services is being raised with increasing frequency. This, in turn, focuses attention on fundamental market structure considerations. It is difficult to see how the PRC can contribute to this dialogue with any particular authority in the absence of a better data-information base.

### Barriers to Successful Accommodation

These case studies illustrate certain recurrent factors besetting commission efforts to accommodate change. They include a chronic data-information gap, an inability to engage in long-term planning which includes a recognition of public requirements, and a failure to serve as custodians of the public interest in the face of conflicting signals for change. In addition, commissions appear to lack the perspective needed to include all of the important variables bearing on performance in the industries under their jurisdiction. This myopia is particularly evident in the case of market structure. Regulators seem to be unable to grasp how market structure can condition the outcome of their decisions, on the one hand; or how market structure can be employed as a regulatory variable to induce change on the other. Finally, regulation's record seems to be particularly uninspired insofar as the ability to innovate in the area of new regulatory concepts and tools is concerned. This dearth of ability to innovate is matched by a parallel inability to implement new concepts as the occasion demands. Of course, these criticisms do not apply equally to all agencies. The FCC seems to have been more successful than have most others in avoiding such pitfalls.

There are a number of reasons for this lack of accomplishment. First, the most important factor is the willingness of commissions to continue to accept the passive review function *vis-à-vis* management in most critical areas. This gives management the initiative over changes in prices or rates, investment, financing, the introduction and abandonment of service, and new directions for research and marketing. Admittedly, regulating agencies have broad authority in each of these areas, but their willingness to accept the posture of passive review severely circumscribes their ability to employ these powers in an affirmative fashion to establish goals, standards or public interest objectives.

Recognition of the importance of the passive review function also provides a useful explanation for the lack of commission planning, the inadequate data-information base, and the hesitancy with respect to innovation in rate-making. The initiative in these areas traditionally goes to management; and regulators typically are content to devise information systems to serve a review-audit function rather than a forward-planning function. Hence, the uniform systems of accounts and the concept of the test year become major regulatory tools for social control, even though they possess obvious limitations for future-oriented actions. These systems of control, in turn, tend to stifle new thinking and new concepts which involve departures from passive review.

Second, there is an excessive reliance on heavily judicialized proceedings to arrive at decisions. Too often, this focuses a disproportionate amount of attention on building a record and too little attention on factors that may have great relevance to the public interest in the long run. Yet, these factors will go largely unnoticed if there is no aggressive protagonist to champion their cause.

Third, there is a tendency for adversary hearings to dominate the behavior and values of those involved. The result is to attach a high importance to discrediting the arguments, testimony and witnesses of the opposition whether that opposition is the utility or carrier, the intervenors or the commission staff. In effect, the outcome is much like that of trench warfare in World War I. It devours the resources and energy of both staff and top management without any demonstrable payoff in territory gained. Further, it diverts the agencies' efforts from the planning function and creates an atmosphere of mutual suspicion and hostility between parties.

A legalistic bias and reliance on adversary proceedings also serves to explain another aspect of the data-information gap. It is in management's interest, at least in the short run, to volunteer little or no information and to resist aggressively any attempt by the agency to extend the frontiers of data gathering. The most expedient response for management is to insist that the cost of collection would be monumental and that the information gained would be of little or no value if collected. This is the most secure route given the fact that it may be used in future hearings and cross-examination. But the data-information gap goes beyond this and ties back to the lack of affirmative planning. Given a passive role, most regulatory agencies simply do not know what information to request and in what form to ask for it.[40]

Fourth, regulators typically lack the resources sufficient to carry out many of the programs needed to accommodate or initiate change.[41] However, it would be a mistake to assume that an increase in budget for them *per se* would do the job. A sense of complacency insofar as the validity of traditional regulatory techniques is concerned provides ample demonstration that something more is needed.

Fifth, a new sense of social legitimacy and a better delineation of the Congressional mandate is needed if regulation is to utilize its resources in a creative fashion. Appearances of agency heads before Congress seldom require that the chairman set forth national policy objectives, as perceived by his agency, and how successful that particular commission has been in achieving these goals.

There are, of course, other barriers to successful accommodation to change. Some argue that the regulatory agency has been handicapped because it proceeds as a collegial body groping forward by consensus on a case-by-case basis. Others argue that supposed political independence is a handicap because it divorces the agency from its basis of popular support.[42]

As an alternative, some reformers have argued that responsibilities should be more centralized and that policy-making should be transferred to the Executive Branch.[43] There is no overwhelming evidence that this type of change would be successful. The Executive Branch has not shown that it can do an outstanding job in this area. Those who think otherwise would be advised to review the meager accomplishments of the Office of Telecommunications Policy in the area of common carrier regulation over the period 1969-1972, and contrast this record with that of the FCC during the same period. The very political pressures which Marver Bernstein viewed as a source of support in 1955 appear to have rendered OTP largely ineffectual.[44] Indeed, the time seems to have come to revisit the early progressives' ideal of an independent body of experts and try to devise procedures which will assure that such a group will be made to perform as originally envisioned.

### Toward a Positive Program for Improvement

There appear to be several sets of conditions that must be satisfied if regulation's capacity to accommodate change and promote the public interest is going to show discernible improvement.

The first step requires the abandonment of the traditional posture of passive review. This involves a realignment of emphasis and priorities. More attention must be given to forecasting and anticipating change, to estimating the social benefits and costs of alternative courses of action, and to inducing change that is desirable and putting constraints on change that is deemed undesirable. The thrust should be in the direction of making regulatory bodies into forward-looking bodies with affirmative action programs.

This means a relative subordination of the adjudicatory function, but not an abandonment of its responsibilities in those areas where quasi-judicial procedures are necessary to the proper discharge of the agency's duties. Rather, it is a matter of a shift in emphasis, with much more attention to policy formulation.

Nor does this change mean that an agency should be excused from accountability. In addition to judicial review, the commission should be held much more accountable to the legislature. Legislatures should require that regulatory agencies develop explicit long-term plans for the industries under their jurisdiction and report on a periodic basis what steps have been taken to implement these objectives. Accountability should even extend to a justification for the continuation of existing patterns of regulation.

It would also be a mistake to assume that planning requires that a regulatory czar impose authoritarian targets and rigid controls on industry. Quite the contrary, proper planning should be continuously aware of alternatives, shifts in national requirements, structural rigidities in industry organization, and outdated public policies that impede accommodation to change. Indeed, assuring maximum flexibility and adaptability as well as pluralism in market structure should be a crucial objective for social control.

Transforming commissions from passive review bodies to affirmative planning agencies can probably be accomplished by Congressional or legislative directive.

Successful accommodation to change also requires consideration of a second set of conditions. These pertain to the need to expand the frontiers of regulatory knowledge. If there has not been a satisfying economic assessment of creamskimming and entry in postal services and communications, or a satisfactory analysis of the infirmities of relying on gradual field price escalation in the gas industry, part of the fault lies in the failure to develop a sufficiently comprehensive conceptual framework capable of delineating and handling all of the important variables. By the same token, a broadened framework is equally necessary for the future where improved accommodation to change requires not only the estimation of the social benefits and costs of alternative courses of action but also an understanding of the factors that can induce desired change and constrain undesired change. The same conclusion holds if regulation is going to prescribe performance standards and then seek to implement their attainment through its various controls over price, earnings, investment, service and entry.

It can be argued, of course, that much attention has already been devoted to subjects such as revenue requirements, cost allocations, and rate structure design. Also, at a more abstract level, increasing attention has been devoted to refinements in peak-load pricing, risk measurement and the cost of capital, tests for cross-subsidization and the theory of the regulated firm.

Yet all of this work suffers from a number of deficiencies insofar as its application to a broadened conceptual framework for regulation is concerned. Much of this research proceeds on the assumption that the firm is a natural monopoly in the classical sense and that it acts as a monopolist in the sale of its output and as a perfectly competitive buyer in its factor or input markets. Such assumptions become increasingly more suspect with the passage of time, as demonstrated in the three case studies discussed earlier.

In addition, there has not been sufficient complementary research in other regulatory areas, which is vital to a full appreciation of the adequacy of earnings controls and pricing practices. For example, there has been relatively little work done on the relationship between incentives and penalties and behavioral motivation, the importance of market structure as a regulatory variable, and the nature and magnitude of positive and negative externalities associated with the provision of public utility services.

Finally, there has been little research on the interdependence among each of these regulatory variables, and particularly the extent to which a significant change in one factor will seriously influence or affect one or more of the other factors.

What emerges, therefore, is an important need to complement a mandate for commission planning with intensive research on relatively unexplored areas of regulation. It is not necessary to start with a blank slate; much information is already in existence, in varying degrees of sophistication, to provide insights for further research.

This can be demonstrated by considering the market-structure variable. The three case studies discussed earlier indicate a number of possible hypotheses or inferences that are susceptible to further analysis as part of the development of a theory of market structure and performance uniquely applicable to the public utility industries.[4,5] The following observations may be illustrative of such inferences.

First, a relaxation of legal restrictions on entry creates the threat of potential entry which may have more significant effects than actual entry and any consequent changes in market structure. The Carterfone decision has precipitated a strong response on the part of established carriers insofar as rates and marketing practices are concerned, so that there appears to be a marked tendency toward cost-based pricing in terminal equipment with more options open to the consumer. Similarly, MCI's entry in the private line market elicited a dramatic series of proposals to restructure rates to reflect departures from system-wide rate averaging for bulk offerings. Yet after more than four years, the change in market concentration in communications is virtually imperceptible. However, the evidence of changes in corporate behavior appear to be very significant.[46]

Second, a market structure that appears at first to be becoming more competitive because of "second-generation" entrants can be deceptive. Once established, new entrants will resist "third-generation" entrants with vigor, employing both commission regulation and other strategies to block entry. United Parcel Service's tactics to foreclose American Delivery Systems from the small parcel market provide an excellent illustration of this practice.[47] The result is that competition, or more correctly, rivalry, is not a self-reinforcing force in such highly imperfect markets and that regulatory alertness is a prerequisite for maintaining flexibility.

Third, an entrenched, monolithic market structure, combined with regulatory acquiescence, gives the dominant firm an opportunity to administer the rate of innovation rather than having such changes market-determined. Conversely, the greater the number and diversity of operating units, the greater the probability that changes in regulatory policy will be translated into creative and diverse types of new tariffs and services for consumers. The innovative tariff changes of Rochester Telephone in the wake of Carterfone provide ample evidence of the importance of decentralized decision making by independent firms. This appears to be a requisite for workable regulation, and the view is hardly new. Paraphrasing B.H. Meyer's comments in 1906, competition alone is inadequate; but regulation requires a number of companies acting independently to be successful.[48]

Fourth, pricing principles are not neutral, but rather have an integral relationship to the structural setting within which they function. The Bell System advocated LRIC to obtain flexibility in order to meet prospective competition; the consortium of gas pipelines sponsoring the Cove Point Project vigorously resisted LRIC on the grounds that it would jeopardize the sales of imported LNG by asking consumers to pay the high incremental cost of Algerian gas. Rather, this group advocated rolled-in prices that averaged the cost of Algerian gas with low-cost flowing gas in order to minimize the risk attendant with the project. It is not surprising, therefore, that the pricing principles advocated correlate with the objectives of the firm.[49]

Fifth, traditionally the fear has been expressed that regulation will seek to preserve a given number of firms on the ground that this results in maintaining adequate service. This belief is unsupported by the case studies of the communications and natural gas industries. On the contrary, the FCC disavowed such a policy in its 1971 statement on entry and competition among specialized carriers.[50] A more important concern is that regulation will equate the existence of two or more firms with the existence of competition. Effective regulatory accommodation to change requires far more attention to collusive behavior, devices to circumvent both regulation and antitrust (such as the formation of holding companies), and vertical, horizontal and conglomerate diversification. The existence of a given number of firms is no assurance that these problems can be dismissed.

Of course, there are a number of critics who doubt that regulation can move aggressively on these fronts and who are skeptical that it can develop the necessary concepts. Yet, in historical perspective there are grounds for optimism. The early progressives' attempts at regulation marked a pioneering application of rudimentary economic principles and quantitative techniques to the social control of business. This experiment also resulted in the development of a data-information base in the years prior to World War I that far exceeded anything available at that time. That this experiment in social intervention has faltered badly in the intervening decades should not deter a new generation of social scientists from picking up the challenge.

**NOTES TO CHAPTER THREE**

1. For a broad discussion of new communications technology stemming from Government sponsored R&D, see: President's Task Force on Communications Policy, *The Roles of the Federal Government in Telecommunications* (Staff Papers, 1969), pp. 23-29.

2. *Allocation of Frequencies in the Bands Above 890 Mc.*, 27 FCC 359 (1959).

3. *Use of the Carterfone Device in Message Toll Telephone Service*, 13 FCC 2d 420 (1968). *In re Application of Microwave Communications Inc. for Construction Permits to Establish New Facilities in the Domestic Public Point to Point Microwave Radio Service at Chicago, Illinois, St. Louis, Missouri, and Intermediate Points*, FCC Docket No. 16509, Decision, August 14, 1969.

4. *Before the FCC in the Matter of Establishment of Policies and Procedures for Consideration of Applications to Provide Specialized Common Carrier Services in the Domestic Public Point-to-Point Microwave Radio Service and Proposed Amendments to Parts 21, 43 and 61 of the Commission's Rules*, First Report and Order, 1971.

5. *Establishment of Domestic Communications-Satellite Facilities by Nongovernmental Entities*, Memorandum, Opinion and Order, FCC Docket No. 16495, March 22, 1972. Also, See: *Telecommunications Reports*, December 26, 1972, pp. 1 et seq., for revisions in final decision.

## A Critique of Regulatory Accommodation to Change 61

6. FCC policy with respect to international satellite communications constitutes a separate study of regulatory efforts to allocate markets and maintain a balance between different technologies. For a detailed discussion see: K.B. Stanley, "The International Telecommunications Industry: Interdependence of Market Structure and Performance Under Regulation." Paper presented at the meetings of the Economics Society of Michigan, April 6, 1973.

7. In August, 1972, the New York Public Service Commission permitted the Rochester Telephone Company to allow the interconnection of customer owned and maintained equipment. Rochester Telephone had initiated this step in the direction of liberalized interconnection, requiring only a simple interface device to protect the network. In granting approval, the Commission noted that this change would advance the movement against the monopoly of supply of terminal equipment (94 PUR 3d 370). Shortly thereafter, the California Commission found that the charges imposed by the General Telephone Company of California for permission to attach a call diverter, via a coupler, to the telephone network were anticompetitive and therefore unlawful (97 PUR 3d 113).

8. See: *Telecommunications Reports*, March 5, 1973, pp. 2-7.

9. See: *Telecommunications Reports*, January 17, 1972, pp. 10-13.

10. The FCC has ruled that telephone carriers cannot own cable television companies in the same geographical area in which the carrier provides telephone service. See: *In The Matter of Applications of Telephone Companies for Section 214 Certificates for Channel Facilities Furnished to Affiliated Community Antenna Television Systems*, FCC Docket No. 18509, January 28, 1970. As a result of its computer inquiry, the FCC has stated that transactions between independent telephone companies and their data affiliates are to be banned and foreclosed. Data affiliates are not regulated by the FCC, but the regulated common carrier services and non-regulated data services are effectively compartmentalized. See: *In the Matter of Regulatory and Policy Problems Presented by the Interdependence of Computer and Communication Service and Facilities*. FCC Docket No. 16979, Final Decision, 1971.

11. After the Carterfone decision (1968), a controversy arose as to whether foreign attachments might impair systemic integrity, and if so what safeguards should be taken. The National Academy of Sciences studied the problem and concluded (in 1970) that a program of equipment certification was one possible answer. Subsequently, Dittberner Associates studied the problem and concluded (1970) that equipment certification was both feasible and desirable. As a follow-up, the FCC co-sponsored a PBX committee to study interconnection standards and procedures. What still remains to come from a study of interconnection is a clear picture of social benefits and costs, including consideration of revenue diversion from carriers but also offsetting cost savings, accelerated innovation and broadened consumer choice.

12. It is also popular to attribute the alleged energy crisis to FPC regulation of the field prices for natural gas. For example, *Business Week* argued that low gas prices discouraged exploration, and that curtailment of pipeline deliveries triggered ". . . shortages of fuel oil as utilities and other industries denied their gas supplies began gobbling up oil. Then as refiners strained late into

the winter to churn out fuel oil, they delayed building up gasoline supplies for the spring and summer when gasoline is most heavily used. So gasoline is now (1973) running short." *Business Week*, April 21, 1973, p. 51.

13. This period begins with the FPC's Natural Gas Investigation which, although authorized in 1944, was begun intensively at the end of the war. The investigation produced two conflicting reports. The Smith-Wimberly Report (1948) which recommended against field price regulation, and the Olds-Draper Report (1948) which favored explicit field regulation. The period closed with the United States Supreme Court giving the FPC jurisdiction over field prices. Phillips Petroleum Co. v. Wisconsin 347 U.S. 672 (1954).

14. This period extends from the Phillips Case through the FPC's decision in the Permian Case establishing the area pricing concept. The decision included a two-price system designed to encourage exploration through higher rates for new gas and curb economic rents through lower rates on flowing gas. Re Permian Basin Area Rates, 34 FPC 159 (1965).

15. The period covers the years from the Permian Case through 1968, which saw the refinement and extension of the area concept to other fields such as Southern Louisiana.

16. See: *Optional Procedure for Certificating New Producer Sales of Natural Gas.* FPC Docket No. R-441. Notice of Proposed Rulemaking and Statement of Policy, April 6, 1972.

17. An F/P ratio of less than 1.0 means that net additions to reserves are less than net production on an annual basis, thereby reducing aggregate year-end reserves. All data apply to United States natural gas supply, excluding Alaska. Source: American Gas Association.

18. Some indication of the impact of secular price increases on reserves can be gained from a letter addressed to the Secretary of the FPC by Senator Philip A. Hart, dated April 27, 1972: "There are vast reserves not yet committed to the interstate market and thus without a price yet put on them . . . If we estimate the uncommitted reserves at a very conservative 1,000 trillion cubic feet, a one-cent increase lifts their value by $10 billion."

For the reluctant producer, the ultimate ceiling price for gas could be fixed by the price of liquified and synthetic natural gas. At present, the delivered city-gate prices for LNG and SNG are more than double the delivered price for newly committed natural gas reserves.

19. "The National Energy Crisis - Revisited." Remarks by John N. Nassikas, Chairman, Federal Power Commission, before the National Press Club, Washington, D.C., April 10, 1973.

20. In 1971, the largest 22 domestic producers sold nearly 71% of the gas supplied to interstate markets. Federal Power Commission, *Sales by Producers of Natural Gas to Interstate Pipeline Companies, 1971*, S-224, October, 1972.

21. See: W.R. Hughes and F.E. Francis, "Regulation and the Energy Crisis," in *A Critique of Administrative Regulation of Public Utilities*, edited by W.J. Samuels and H.M. Trebing, East Lansing: 1972, p. 233.

22. To the extent that pipelines hold extensive gas reserves, such countervailing power is further reduced.

23. The endorsement of oil import quotas by the Chairman of the FPC on the grounds that high oil prices would alleviate the gas shortage by encouraging domestic exploration for oil and gas has been challenged by Paul MacAvoy. He argues that high oil prices, supported by import quotas, increase the demand for gas and contribute to the shortage. See: P.W. MacAvoy, "The Regulation-Induced Shortage of Natural Gas," *Journal of Law and Economics*, April, 1971, p. 170.

24. For a detailed description of the scope of the Survey as well as other FPC actions pertaining to the gas shortage, see: Statement of John N. Nassikas, Chairman, Federal Power Commission, Hearings Before the Joint Economic Committee of the United States Congress, June 8, 1972.

25. Interestingly, the Olds-Draper Report (*op. cit.*) set forth some of the basic elements of regulatory planning as early as 1948 in its recommendation that the FPC fix the field prices of gas. These included an independent gas survey capable of providing continuous information on markets and reserves, and a recognition that fixing prices required administrative allocation of gas between superior and inferior uses.

26. *Towards Postal Excellence*, The Report of the President's Commission on Postal Organization, Washington: 1968.

27. Postal Reorganization Act of 1970. Pub. L. No. 91-375 (Aug. 12, 1970).

28. These conditions apply more appropriately to LRIC; however, a subsequent Postal witness argued that differences in practice between SRIC, as estimated by USPS, and LRIC were not large. See: PRC Docket R71-1, Tr. 7917.

29. Arguments in favor of economies of scale were made on the basis of simple judgments or speculation. For a bibliography of other cost studies of the postal system as well as an econometric analysis that refutes the case for economies of scale, see: R.E. Stevenson, *Postal Pricing Problems and Productivity Function*. Unpublished Ph.D. dissertation, Michigan State University, 1973.

30. Mathematica estimated that the inelastic demand values ranging from .170 to less than .003 would remain valid for second-class mail increases up to 200 percent over 1970 rate levels. The USPS proposed increase for regular rate second-class publications was 145.4 percent. Mathematica estimated that the inelastic demand value for third-class mail of .368 would remain valid for price increases up to 50 percent over 1970 rate levels. The USPS proposed increase for the third-class bulk rate was 28.5 percent. See: Mathematica, *A Study of the Demand for Advertising, Newspaper, and Magazine Mail*, 1971.

31. The question of pricing principles or standards was to be approached through an invitation to submit suggestions on the relevant data that should be collected . . . to make these determinations." See: *Postal Rate and Fee Increases, 1971*. PRC Docket No. R71-1, Opinion and Recommended Decision, June 5, 1972, pp. 61-62.

32. The first National Service Goal was introduced in 1971 for air mail. It is allegedly the first time that postal management formally established delivery goals of this type. See: PRC Docket R71-1, Tr. 2811.

*64  Regulation in Further Perspective*

33. The complete postal operation involves three time phases or segments: (1) collection time (point of drop to cancellation); (2) processing time (cancellation to carrier for sequencing to addresses); (3) delivery time (exit point to addressee). NSI is concerned only with processing time. *Ibid.*, Tr. 1481.

34. *Ibid.*, Tr. 1496-1497.

35. *Ibid.*, Tr. 2763, 3870.

36. *Ibid.*, Tr. 12,253.

37. A confrontation between the USPS and the PRC over data and information for postal reclassification can already be anticipated. See: *Wall Street Journal*, May 3, 1973, p. 3.

38. Unlike the subsequent Commission decision, the Chief Examiner attached great importance to the need to establish ratemaking principles at the earliest possible date. Examiner Wenner's decision provides an excellent critique of alternative postal pricing theories as a point of departure for further action. See: *Postal Rate and Fee Increases, 1971*, PRC Docket No. R71-1, Chief Examiner's Initial Decision on Postal Rate and Fee Increases, February 3, 1972.

39. The PRC rejected this role. See: Opinion and Recommended Decision, *op. cit.*, pp. 257-260. If the agency does eventually accept this role, it will have to consider a number of difficult problems. Should penalties be imposed on the USPS for waste, mismanagement, and failure to attain service goals? And if so, does the consumer bear the incidence of these failings regardless of the action taken by the regulator?

40. With the emergence of a new market structure characterized by an admixture of monopoly and competition, a new barrier to the gathering of data and information can be expected to develop. This is the alleged need for privacy on the grounds that more information will give an undue advantage to non-regulated rivals.

41. The limited budget of the FCC's Common Carrier Bureau provides an excellent illustration. Between 1935 and 1971, AT&T's assets have grown 1000 percent, its revenues have grown 2000 percent, and its net income has increased over 4000 percent. In contrast, the Common Carrier Bureau had a staff of 300 assigned to its special telephone investigation in the mid-1930s; its total staff in 1971 was 155. The budget is also less today, in real terms, for the Bureau than the funds appropriated by Congress in 1935-1937 for the special telephone investigation. See: "Opening the Communications Market." Address by A.H. Ende, Deputy Chief, Common Carrier Bureau, FCC, before the Electro Science Analyst Group, February 15, 1973.

42. M.H. Bernstein, *Regulating Business by Independent Commission*, Princeton: 1955.

43. For a survey of major reform proposals, see: M.H. Bernstein, "Independent Regulatory Agencies: A Perspective on Their Reform," in Samuels and Trebing, *op. cit.*, pp. 3-23.

44. This criticism focuses exclusively on the ability of OTP to induce major changes in policy and performance in the common carrier field. For example, OTP proposed a policy of liberalized entry into domestic satellites, but a reading of the FCC's 1972 decision (see note 5, above) does not disclose that this declaration had any significant impact on the decision. Indeed, the FCC

appears to have been influenced much more by its own past policies of liberalized entry.

45. For a further discussion, see: W.G. Shepherd, "Entry as a Substitute for Regulation," *American Economic Review*, May 1973, pp. 98-105.

46. See: S.E. Bonsack, "Marketing Functions in Telecommunications under Conditions of Growing Competition," and D.R. Casey, "Marketing and Planning Problems in the Independent Telephone Industry," papers presented at Institute of Public Utilities Conference, April 24-25, 1973, East Lansing, Michigan.

47. See: Motion of U.S. Department of Justice for Leave to Intervene and Petition for Reconsideration. *American Delivery Systems, Inc., Freight Forwarder Application*, ICC Docket No. FF-376, May 16, 1972.

48. B.H. Meyer, *A History of the Northern Securities Case*, Bulletin of the University of Wisconsin, Madison: 1906.

49. For a further discussion, see: H.M. Trebing, "Common Carrier Regulation—the Silent Crisis," *Law and Contemporary Problems*, Spring, 1969, pp. 310-322.

50. See note 4, above.

Chapter Four

# The Averch-Johnson Hypothesis after Ten Years

Leland L. Johnson

Ten years ago Harvey Averch and I developed a model of the firm's behavior under the constraint that the return on capital investment not exceed a given level, specified by a governmental regulatory body. Major assumptions of the model are that (a) the firm seeks to maximize profit, (b) the market cost of capital is constant, (c) the allowable or "fair" rate of return exceeds the cost of capital, and (d) no regulatory lag exists. Under these assumptions the model leads to conclusions that the capital-labor ratio is greater than that which would minimize cost at the level of output selected by the firm, and that the firm may have an incentive to serve competitive markets even if revenues fall below incremental cost in those markets, with the difference more than compensated by increased net revenues permitted through price increases in its monopoly services.[*]

This formulation has attracted numerous comments, critiques, and replies; but virtually all the discussion has remained on theoretical grounds. Unfortunately, little empirical analysis has appeared to suggest the importance of these distortions in the real world. The purpose of this paper is briefly to note major developments in the theory, to examine bits of evidence that have come to light, and to address possibilities for further empirical work.

### Developments in the Theory

One major thrust has involved geometrical treatments of the distortion in the use of inputs as an alternative to the mathematical formulation in our model. In particular, the formulation of E.E. Zajac has served as a point of departure for much subsequent theoretical analysis.

---

[*]Views expressed in this paper are those of the author. They should not be interpreted as reflecting the views of The Rand Corporation or the official opinion or policy of any of its governmental or private research sponsors. The comments of R.E. Park on an earlier draft are gratefully acknowledged.

Much of this paper appeared in the May, 1973 *American Economic Review*.

A second thrust has involved rigorous analysis of propositions that do and do not necessarily flow from our model. This is illustrated by a paper in which William Baumol and Alvin Klevorick demonstrate among other things (a) that the capital-labor ratio of the regulated firm is not necessarily larger than that of the unconstrained profit-maximizing monopolist although, as noted above, the capital-labor ratio is excessive for the regulated firm at the output it selects; (b) that (following Fred Westfield and Akira Takayama) the distortion may increase rather than decrease as the allowable rate of return approaches the market cost of capital from above, and (c) that the output of the regulated firm is not necessarily greater than that of the profit-maximizing monopolist, depending on the nature of substitutability among inputs of labor and capital.

The most extensive synthesis of the literature to date, together with many original contributions, is contained in a study by Elizabeth Bailey. With respect to point (c) above, she demonstrates that the output of the regulated firm would rise above that of the profit-maximizing firm except in the unusual circumstance in which capital is an inferior input—a situation in which an increase in output is accompanied by a decrease in capital input. Among the many other interesting aspects of her study is clarification of the distinction between productive and wasteful use of capital. The so-called Averch-Johnson effect of overcapitalization does not as a general case involve "gold-plating" or purchase of plant solely to be held idle; rather, as Bailey demonstrates, the firm seeks to derive whatever additional revenue is obtainable through overcapitalization. The firm would take into account the marginal product of capital in deciding among alternative investments. Only in the unusual circumstance where the marginal physical product of capital falls below zero would the firm be led to gold-plate or to hold capital strictly idle as a way of taking further advantage of unexploited monopoly power to increase its profit. The firm, therefore, would have an incentive to reduce rather than to increase the acquisition cost of new capital facilities, because a lower cost would permit it to invest in yet new directions (but still at an excessive capital-labor ratio) and achieve yet higher levels of profits within a given regulatory constraint. For this reason, as Bailey points out, it is only under special conditions that a firm would have an incentive to collude with its suppliers to increase equipment cost and hence expand its rate base, as has been suggested by Westfield.

A third thrust has involved the effects of a wide range of alternative assumptions on the behavior of the regulated firm. A leading example is again the study by Bailey in which the consequences of regulatory lag, increasing cost of capital, alternatives to profit-maximizing behavior, peak-load demand conditions, and other possibilities are examined. The behavior of the firm, including tendencies toward undercapitalization as well as toward overcapitalization, can be greatly affected, depending on the inclusion of such alternative assumptions.

In light of the extensive discussion over the past decade, it seems fair to say that the Averch-Johnson analysis, given its assumptions, remains valid on theoretical grounds. But the question remains about the importance of overcapitalization and cross-subsidization in reality. Are the Averch-Johnson effects merely an intellectual curiosity, or do they describe serious distortions in the behavior of regulated firms? Unfortunately the answer is not clear. It is not sufficient to compare the behavior of regulated and unregulated firms because, as mentioned above, the capital-labor ratio of the regulated firm is not necessarily greater than that of the unregulated monopolist. The search for gold-plating and obviously wasteful use of capital is likely to prove fruitless since, within the regulatory constraint, the firm does seek to use capital in a manner that produces additional revenue.

To the extent that Averch-Johnson effects operate, they do so subtly: the firm can engage in activities for a number of reasons that seem plausible; to separate the real reasons from the merely plausible is not easy. For example, the firm may prefer to buy rather than to lease facilities on the grounds that to do so permits it greater control over the reliability, availability, and use of the facilities. The fact that owned, not leased, equipment goes into the rate base may also play a role—one strong enough to encourage the firm to opt for owning rather than leasing, despite the fact that the latter might be socially more efficient. As another example, the firm may have a choice between two kinds of equipment—one relatively expensive but requiring small maintenance charges, the other less costly but with heavier recurring costs. The first may be selected on the grounds that uncertainty about the level and reliability of variable inputs (perhaps because of possible wage increases and labor strikes) renders the choice wise. But the greater contribution of the former to rate base can play an important, if hidden, role in biasing the decision. Or the firm may cut prices in markets threatened by competitive entry with assertions that it can perform the service more efficiently than competitors without burdening its monopoly services; yet it may engage in competitive rate cutting more aggressively than would be the case were the additional capital requirements for the competitive services not included in the rate base on which tariffs for its monopoly services are established.

### Empirical Evidence

But the basic question remains of how important these factors are in the real world, and the extent to which empirical investigation over the last decade has contributed to the answer.

Unfortunately, most of the existing empirical work has been of a casual sort. Cases in which the firm behaves in a manner consistent with the A-J propositions can also be explained in terms of other considerations. A problem with so much empirical analysis in this area is that firms can pursue particular activities for a number of reasons—some real, others merely plausible. To separate the real from the merely plausible is not easy.

For example, some of the earlier evidence was cited by Professor

Wein in a book edited by Harry Trebing. Wein noted that the National Power Survey showed the electric power industry to have about 25 percent more generating capacity than the expected annual peak load in 1963. He suggested that this was explainable in terms of A-J effects. A commentator on Wein's paper, William Hughes, pointed out that, while A-J effects may have been a contributing factor, other forces also were at work. Professor Wein goes on to mention William Shepherd's observation that the rates of return in telephone service vary from individual cities from a positive 7.22 percent, to a minus 6.87 percent in smaller towns.

Why does the regulated firm embrace rate averaging where underlying costs per customer are quite different between small towns and cities? One possibility—in line with the second aspect of the A-J effect of entering markets whose revenues do not cover incremental costs—is that the firm is willing to take losses in the small towns as a means of expanding the rate base. While the behavior of rate averaging is consistent with the A-J propositions, telephone executives deny it in favor of another, also plausible, argument: that it is beneficial to develop telephone service in small towns because to do so increases the value of the service to the large city users who are enabled to communicate with more people. By subsidizing the small town user to take into account this external effect, everyone benefits.

I have some problems with this "externalities" argument, but I will not go into them now, except to say that rate averaging causes rates to be higher in cities than otherwise would be the case, thereby reducing the number of telephone connections in the cities. It is not obvious on *a priori* grounds that rate averaging increases the *total* number of customers that would determine the value of service to individual subscribers.

The only systematic quantitative analysis of the potential magnitude of overcapitalization of which I am aware is a study by E.D. Emery. Examining privately owned class A and B steam electric power plants in the United States during the period 1961-1965, he considers distortions arising when the private cost of capital—the "planning" cost—to the firm is less than the market or social cost, with the disparity arising as a consequence of the allowable rate of return rising above the market cost. In one case he assumes that the planning cost is 85 percent of market cost; in a second case, he assumes 75 percent.

In the first case he estimates the range of annual social welfare loss at about $12 million to $24 million depending on assumptions about the prices of factor inputs; in the second he estimates a loss at $59 million to $104 million. A major problem with this analysis is that the planning figures of 85 percent and 75 percent are only assumed. The extent to which planning figures do vary from market costs remains unknown. In any event, the disparity undoubtedly varies a good deal from industry to industry and from one time to another.

Still, Emery's approach is an interesting point of departure for examining the costs and benefits of regulation. He goes on to estimate the gross welfare gains of regulation of from $20 million to $42 million and $71 million to $222 million respectively for planning costs of 85 percent and 75 percent of market cost. The salient result is that overcapitalization can eat up a substantial proportion of welfare gains from regulation: the lower bound welfare gain of $20 million could be reduced to only $8 million, while the upper bound of $224 could be cut to $120 million, or by nearly one-half. Emery concludes that although on balance consumers do benefit from regulation, the net benefits are so small that one wonders whether the gain outweighs the cost of regulation in terms of budgets of public utility commissions, litigation expenses and, of course, fees to economists who are brought in by so many parties as consultants.

Other evidence, of a causal sort, suggests that in some cases firms do have an incentive to expand rate base. A leading example is the long controversy that arose in the mid-1960s over the ownership of earth terminals to be used with communications satellites for international telephone, television, and other services. The Communications Satellite Corporation (Comsat), AT&T, Hawaiian Telephone, and the international telegraph or "record" carriers all sought to construct and operate earth terminals to be used with satellites under the control of Comsat. A leading argument used to support ownership of ground stations by the terrestrial common carriers was that this was important to ensure "systemic integrity"—the requirement that the entire communications systems be operated as a well-integrated unit where, so to speak, the communication chain is only as strong as the weakest link. In any event, the international communications system is fragmented. By law, Comsat has a monopoly in the control of the satellites themselves, in cooperation with the international satellite consortium, Intelsat; the terrestrial carriers have their own land-line facilities to serve final users; and the satellite earth stations are left in the middle.

After a long debate, the FCC decided to authorize joint ownership where in most cases Comsat would cover 50 percent of ground station investment; AT&T another percentage, and other entities, including the telegraph or "record" carriers, another percentage, depending largely on their relative use of satellite facilities.

I will mention a few figures to show you how this decision was made in 1965. The ground stations were divided into three categories: those that are in the conterminous states, those in Hawaii, and those in Puerto Rico and the Virgin Islands. The FCC decided that in all cases Comsat would own one-half of each. In the conterminous states AT&T would have 28.5 percent and three record carriers would have, respectively, 7 percent, 10.5 percent and 4 percent ownership. In the case of Hawaii and Puerto Rico-Virgin Islands, the percentages were somewhat different.

This case illustrates not only the possible operation of the A-J effect but also how the FCC goes about making decisions. When Professor Dewey quoted Professor Knight earlier in this collection to the effect that regulation is largely a matter of conflict resolution, he made a point that certainly is true with respect to the FCC. Here, as elsewhere, the FCC continued its long standing habit of compromise which might be crudely expressed, "How can you satisfy the largest number of important claimants without making anybody too awfully unhappy?"

At this writing, eight ground terminals are employed by United States carriers for international service, representing a gross investment of about $68 million. One is owned solely by Comsat; the rest are owned jointly by one or more terrestrial carriers along with Comsat. In the absence of incentives to expand rate base, it is difficult to explain why terrestrial carriers would be so concerned about ownership of satellite ground terminals. In any event, ownership would not affect their market shares or competitive relationships, since only they and not Comsat are permitted by law to provide service to final users; and, in any event, access to satellites themselves would be controlled by Comsat.

At the same time, this evidence does not necessarily indicate overcapitalization as a reflection of the Averch-Johnson effect. Rather it illustrates problems that arise in dividing capital facilities among separate entities, where the capital may or may not be used most efficiently with other inputs. To trace possibilities of overcapitalization would involve examination of factor inputs in the design, construction and operation of earth terminals. Nevertheless, this case does suggest that one of the necessary conditions exists under which overcapitalization could arise—a disparity between allowable and market rates of return that generates an incentive to expand rate base.

A second bit of evidence arises when we consider the manner in which costs are treated for installing telephone wiring and terminal equipment on customer premises. In 1972, station connections and disconnections in the Bell system ran to about $1.4 billion, which entered the rate base, in comparison with about $8.8 billion for Bell's total gross addition to plant in that year. A recent study by the Office of Telecommunications Policy (OTP) argues that a onetime compensatory charge to customers for internal wiring, and expensing rather than capitalizing the bulk of station connection charges, would benefit the Bell system in terms of cash flow and tax liabilities. This practice suggested by OTP would produce results closer to those of other utilities where customers do make a onetime outlay for interior connections, and it would also recognize that the revenue-producing characteristics of station connections depend on the changing needs of customers and not on the inherent lifetime characteristics of hardware. According to the OTP study, the degree of uncertainty in the use of station connection installations would argue in favor of expensing the bulk of the cost rather than capitalizing the total and entering it into the rate base.

Given the strong tax and cash flow advantages, according to the OTP estimates, one wonders why Bell has not already adopted this practice—all the more so in light of the difficulty that Bell executives frequently claim in raising the enormous amounts of capital required each year to meet the rapid expansion in demand for telephone service. To follow the recommendations of OTP would dramatically reduce the demand for new capital by shifting some of the burden directly to consumers. In the absence of an incentive to expand rate base, why would the firm not exercise this option to relieve itself of substantial capital requirements? Perhaps the objective of maintaining systemic integrity plays a role, where, with ownership of internal connections in the hands of customers, the firm might have less control over reliability and quality of service. But a fully satisfactory answer, as opposed to conjecture, is elusive.

A third example, again drawn from the telecommunications field, involves the choices United States telecommunications common carriers make between the use of cable and satellite facilities for international services. AT&T and the record carriers share the ownership of transoceanic cables with the investment entering their respective rate bases. Use of satellite circuits, on the other hand, involves leasing facilities from Comsat (although the ownership of earth stations is shared with Comsat as mentioned above). In 1967-68 acrimonious debate arose as to whether the TAT-5 cable proposed by the United States terrestrial carriers between the United States and Europe should be authorized in light of the lower estimated cost of relying on additional satellite capacity provided by Comsat. TAT-5, involving a cost of about $70 million, was eventually authorized and built partly on the justifications set forth by the terrestrial carriers that a "balance" is required between cable and satellite facilities to ensure adequate reliability of service; and that, moreover, the balance ought to be roughly 50-50. (However, one must immediately point out that overall reliability depends more on the number of separate facilities than on the number of kinds of facilities). In 1972, an additional cable, TAT-6, was authorized between the United States and Europe; and at this writing the carriers are requesting authorization to construct a 5000-mile cable from Hawaii to Okinawa, involving an investment of about $122 million, despite the large and rapidly growing capacity in satellite facilities over the Pacific.

Again, it would not be safe to ascribe this behavior solely to rate base considerations. Telecommunications carriers prefer to provide customer service end to end under their purview to facilitate systemic integrity and to avoid relying on outside suppliers over whom they do not have complete control. Also, the lower cost of satellite circuits may not be reflected in the rates charged to terrestrial carriers by virtue of the worldwide averaging practice used in pricing satellite services. Still, if the raising of capital is as difficult as is frequently alleged by public utilities executives, one would expect to observe a preference (or at least neutrality) for leasing rather than owning facilities of the sort involved in the cable-satellite controversy.

In addition to the preceding evidence regarding expansion of rate base, there remains the second aspect of the Averch-Johnson model dealing with cross-subsidization—the incentive of regulated firms to expand into competitive markets even if revenues do not cover incremental costs. Here again empirical evidence is lacking largely because of the extraordinary difficulty of defining and measuring the relevant incremental costs—a subject treated in a particularly useful paper by Harold Wein. Nevertheless, the issue of cross-subsidization is as pressing as it was a decade ago, if not more so. In our 1962 paper, Averch and I noted the debate about the pricing of AT&T's Telepak services in competition with Western Union's private line offerings. The debate eventually culminated in a substantial Telepak rate increase in the late 1960s as has been discussed by William Melody.

Other controversies have arisen, especially in the domestic communications satellite field. Debate has persisted over the last half-dozen years regarding who should be permitted to own and operate satellites and under what conditions satellite services are to be offered. The FCC has recently decided to restrict AT&T to the use of satellites only for its monopoly services on grounds that:

> if AT&T were permitted unrestricted use of satellites for both monopoly and specialized services, this might obscure any meaningful comparison of operating costs between satellite and terrestrial facilities for the provision of specialized services, as well as curtail any realistic opportunity for entry by others, to serve the specialized markets via satellite.
> We (FCC) recognize that the problem of cross-subsidy now exists with respect to the establishment of rates and identification of relevant costs for specialized services furnished by AT&T terrestrially. However, this long-standing problem would be exacerbated by permitting the troublesome monopoly and competitive services combination to be carried over into this new arena. (p. 6.)

Thus, although empirical evidence is lacking regarding the quantitative danger of cross-subsidization in this new field, the fear of cross-subsidization is clearly affecting regulatory decision making.

Of course, many contrary examples to the preceding can be enumerated. Whatever desire regulated firms may have to expand rate base was not enough to prevent the severe shortage of telephone capacity in New York City that arose several years ago and is still being corrected; nor has it prevented the serious shortage of capacity in electric power generation that is a source of increasing social concern; nor is it enough to overcome the reluctance of utilities to adopt environmental controls involving facilities that would add to rate base. Clearly a number of factors are at work that can swamp any tendencies toward overcapitalization—restrictions on power plant siting and building (due to environmental considerations) that in any event would generate a shortage of capacity in the face of rapidly growing demands for energy; errors in forecasting demand for service (as in the New York telephone case); regulatory lags in rate adjustments; and the extent to which regulated firms do in fact have monopoly power that can be exploited through rate increases as described in the Averch-Johnson model.

With respect to regulatory lags, as Bailey and Roger Coleman point out, the longer the firm must wait for an increase in rates to bring the allowable rate of return to a point above the market cost of capital, the less incentive the firm has to add to rate base in the interim; for during the time lag it suffers a loss that only eventually will be compensated.

However, it is useful to distinguish between two kinds of regulatory lags. The first I shall call *Type I* to describe the situation in which the firm is caught in a general inflationary spiral leading eventually to rate increases. This is this kind of lag that would dampen incentives to overcapitalize and is the kind of lag facing so many utilities today as a consequence of the strong inflationary forces that have persisted since the mid-1960s. Under a second kind of lag, which I shall call *Type II*, the firm is able to enjoy technological advances of such magnitude and/or such large economies of scale in the face of growing demand that its unit costs fall in spite of inflationary forces. Such a situation leads eventually to rate decreases rather than increases. It is under Type II lags that one would expect overcapitalization to emerge most clearly. In the extreme case, by sufficient overcapitalization, the firm could remain within the range of a fair rate of return and postpone indefinitely pressures by the regulatory agency to reduce rates.

The differences between the cases in which firms seek to avoid capital investment are, I would conjecture, traceable in part to whether Type I or Type II lags are at work. Today, Type I lags are far more evident than they were a decade ago. Hence the potential for overcapitalization is probably less than it was in 1962 when the Averch-Johnson model was formulated.

Another factor is the extent to which the firm actually has monopoly power. In some cases, there may exist no set of rates under which a reasonable return on capital can be generated. As Merton Peck points out, in 1960 the return on railroad stockholders' equity ran to about 2.2 percent despite the fact that railroads were filing numerous requests for rate increases, to which the ICC did not object. As in the case of Type I lags, the situation is not one conducive to the emergence of Averch-Johnson effects.

**Future Directions for Empirical Analysis**

In conclusion, I would like to make four observations: First, if the A-J effect of overcapitalization or the provision of non-remunerative service exists, it operates subtly. When I have discussed these possibilities with business executives, they scoff; they think the A-J effect describes a situation in which they sit around a room trying to decide how to increase their rate base; and, of course, they don't do that. If the A-J effect operates, it does so in situations such as that of an engineer trying to decide how much back-up capacity to build into a transmitting and receiving system on a microwave tower; everything else remaining equal, he may opt to go to a capacity greater than is socially optimal by virtue of the fact that the cost is capitalized. Or if there is a decision to be made about installing a microwave system that requires little maintenance as opposed to one that requires a good deal of maintenance, the decision may be biased in favor of the one requiring little maintenance, since its higher investment cost goes into the rate base. But these are complicated decisions that can be justified on a number of grounds. To isolate the contribution of rate-base consideration to such decisions is extremely difficult.

Second, a possibility arises of channeling whatever effect rate-base considerations have into socially useful activities. It may be true that the price of capital to the firm does not reflect the market price, but the market price may not be a very good indicator of social value either. There may be externalities at work. For example, in a broader social context it might be desirable that the firm build more excess capacity than would otherwise be the case, provide more reliable service, and go along less reluctantly with environmental controls imposed by the federal government, with the realization that expansion in rate base would be recouped in higher revenues permitted by the regulatory agency.

A leading example can be found in the field of cable television, a rapidly growing industry as discussed by Professor Barnett elsewhere in this book. Although rate-base regulation is not now employed in that industry, it may be introduced as the industry develops. Here a capital intensive bias might be socially beneficial in encouraging the cable operator to build a larger capacity plant than he otherwise would have, were he subject to purely market forces that do not fully reflect social costs and benefits.

Third, in response to Professor Dewey and others, I would like to address the question of deregulation or major changes in regulation. The FCC has reached a number of questionable decisions in the past, as in the case of cable television, along the lines Professor Barnett discusses. But the FCC is much more inclined to open the telecommunications field to competitive forces than was true ten years ago. It is no longer willing to accept uncritically the argument that a natural monopoly exists in all cases, to justify the need for full-blown regulation. The thought is becoming increasingly accepted that there are areas in the telecommunications field where one can have competition, or at least where one should experiment with competition. For that reason, the FCC has adopted a "semi-open skies" policy with respect to the use of domestic satellites, to permit a number of applicants to offer service that would otherwise have been provided, if at all, by the telephone company.

Another leading example was the entry of competing private line services, arising out of the so-called M.C.I. case, where the FCC recently decided to open up the field in private line services to M.C.I., Datran and a number of other groups offering specialized services, mostly to large business users. This, again, raises the question of cross-subsidization. To what extent should Bell be permitted to reduce rates to meet competition, and to what extent would reduction in rates for competitive services raise the danger of burdening the remaining monopoly service?

The FCC has also decided that General Telephone and Electronics may enter the interstate message toll business, through the use of satellites. Message toll has long been considered one of the most "natural" of natural monopolies. Yet, even here, we may see competition. This will be a very interesting case to follow as an illustration of the extent to which competition does bring about socially desirable change—or perhaps only wasteful duplication as conventional wisdom would have it.

Finally, the question arises as to what promising lines of inquiry might be pursued to quantify the distortions in behavior that result from regulatory constraints. It is unlikely to prove fruitful to examine the extent of back-up or standby capacity in cases where the optimum level of such facilities is heavily dependent on subjective judgment about what is required to ensure an "adequate" quality and reliability of service. A more promising, though still limited, approach would involve examining the capital planning cost figures employed by engineers and others in the design and construction of equipment to determine whether biases arise with respect to capital intensity. However the value of this approach is limited to the extent that distortions may be embodied in major, high-level, corporate decisions to enter competing markets at rate levels designed to match or to better those offered by competitors, or to build and own more costly facilities rather than lease less expensive ones, regardless of planning cost factors employed by engineers in lower-level decisions.

Perhaps one of the most promising approaches is to examine the comparative behavior of firms subject to Type I and Type II regulatory lags. Does the evidence show, for example, that firms subject to Type II lags more aggressively enter competitive markets and seek to expand rate bases along the lines described above? Or for a given firm over time, does its behavior differ during periods of Type II lags from that during periods of Type I lags? Although serious problems of *ceteris paribus* enter here (as they do in so much empirical work), investigation distinguishing between types of regulatory lag may be fruitful to providing insight into the quantitative effects of regulatory constraints.

In conclusion, the observations of William R. Hughes, made in 1967, merit reiteration:

> As a first theoretical go-around on an important question, Averch-Johnson merit serious attention. But a good bit more is needed—in more complete theorizing, in thoughtful consideration of influences excluded from our rigorous models, and in empirical work—before we can claim a very firm understanding of the impact of rate of return ceilings on resource allocation. (p. 74)

By this time, five years later, a great deal more has been done in theorizing, and a fair amount has been done in thoughtful consideration going beyond the bounds of formal models. What remains seriously lacking is empirical analysis to give us a better quantitative notion of how the firm is affected under a variety of circumstances encountered in the real world, to provide a sounder basis for assessing the costs and benefits of current regulatory practices, and to evaluate the desirability of alternative regulatory reforms.

**REFERENCES TO CHAPTER FOUR**

Harvey Averch and Leland L. Johnson, "Behavior of the Firm under Regulatory Constraint," *American Economic Review*, December 1962, 52, 1053-69.

Elizabeth E. Bailey, Economic Theory of Regulatory Constraint, unpublished Ph.D. dissertation, Princeton University, 1972.

_____ and Rogert D. Coleman, "The Effect of Lagged Regulation in an Averch-Johnson Model," *Bell Journal of Economics and Management Science*, Spring, 1971, 2, 279-292.

William J. Baumol and Alvin K. Klevorich, "Input Choices and Rate-of-Return Regulation: An Overview of the Discussion," *Bell Journal of Economics and Management Science*, Autumn, 1970, 1, 162-190.

E.D. Emery, An Investigation of the Potential Welfare Effects Associated with Rate of Return Regulation of the Steam-Electric Industry in the United States, unpublished Ph.D. dissertation, University of Minnesota, 1969.

William R. Hughes, "Comment: Fair Rate of Return and Incentives—Some General Considerations," in *Performance under Regulation*, Harry M. Trebing, ed., Michigan State University, 1968.

William H. Melody, "Interservice Subsidy: Regulatory Standards in Applied Economics," in *Essays in Public Utility Pricing and Regulation*, Harry Trebing, ed., Michigan State University, 1971.

Merton J. Peck, "Competitive Policy for Transportation?" in *The Crisis of the Regulatory Commissions*, Paul W. MacAvoy, ed., New York, 1970.

Frederic M. Scherer, *Industrial Market Structure and Economic Performance*, Chicago, 1970.

Akira Takayama, "Behavior of the Firm under Regulatory Constraint," *American Economic Review*, June 1969, 59, 255-60.

Harold H. Wein, *Testimony*, FCC Docket No. 16258, Staff Exhibit No. 50, July 1968.

Fred M. Westfield, "Regulation and Conspiracy," *American Economic Review*, June 1965, 55, 424-443.

Edward E. Zajac, "A Geometric Treatment of Averch-Johnson's Behavior of the Firm Model," *American Economic Review*, March 1970, 60, 117-125.

Federal Communications Commission, "Establishment of Domestic Communications Facilities by Non-Governmental Industries," *Second Report and Order*, Docket 16495, Washington, June 1972.

U.S. Office of Telecommunications Policy, "Station Connection Study," Staff Research Paper, 1972.

Chapter Five

# Perspectives on CATV Regulation

Harold J. Barnett

CATV, or cable television, is a still emerging and only partly formed industry. Its regulation has been in flux. In a decade it has gone from no regulation through freezes and various governmental rules to a lengthy and complex set of regulations adopted by the FCC in 1972 (22, FCC, 1972). The pathways, accelerations, stops, hesitations and details of the journey over the past decade have been very confusing. Sol Schildhause, Director of the CATV Bureau of the FCC, commented in 1969, "We stir, move ahead a step, go sideways for a while, back and fill, re-examine—all the while groping for a permanent policy" (17). Still further changes in both federal and state regulation are likely. In this situation it seems to me that I can serve best by offering perspective judgments on the regulation of cable television. These are my own views on the main happenings and significant present conditions and prospects.*

### Public Policy in Broadcasting

Regulation of CATV cannot be understood without a bit of background on the 50-year history of United States federal regulation of radio and TV.

In the 1920s electronic signal interference in radio broadcasting and receiving became a problem in advanced nations. Public policy decisions became necessary to avoid the difficulty. Britain and continental Europe generally chose to limit supply severely and further opted for monopoly control of broadcasting in the hands of government or quasi-governmental corporations (5, Briggs, 1961, 1965; 7, Coase, 1950; 15, Paulu, 1967). The United States deliberately chose otherwise. Regulation by the Federal Communications Commission (in early years the Federal Radio Commission) would primarily take the form of licensing

---

*I am grateful to the National Science Foundation for financial assistance in my communications and broadcasting research, under Grant No. GS-3510.

*79*

## 80 Regulation in Further Perspective

in order to prevent interference. The larger objective was to open broadcasting to private enterprise, in favor of competition and expansion of supply to the maximum extent possible. There would be no public utility type regulation of prices, rates, profits or programs (14, Jones, 1967).

In subsequent FCC licensing of the limited frequency space, the concepts of competition, localism, and large numbers of suppliers played major roles. For example, the FCC limited the number of high-powered, clear-channel radio broadcasters from major cities, in order to reserve electromagnetic frequencies for larger numbers of local stations. The numbers of stations which might be owned by a single company were limited by FCC rules. FCC fostered the introduction of FM radio, whose frequencies could accommodate large numbers of stations with small individual service areas. In television broadcasting, the FCC encouraged UHF-TV and sponsored the All Channel Receiver Act, which required that all sets have UHF tuners. It also made recurrent efforts to reduce network dominance in program supply, in the interest of competition and localism. Finally, the broadcasting industry is not exempt from anti-trust laws, and the Anti-Trust division of the Department of Justice has prosecuted anti-competitive behavior on a number of occasions.

### Supply Functions

The ineluctable difficulty of television, however, was the supply conditions inherent in technology and the electromagnetic frequency allocations by FCC to the television industry. The over-the-air television supply curves, except in the very largest cities, provide VHF channels for only a few TV stations, and ultimately channel space for half a dozen or fewer VHF and UHF stations; and small cities are even more limited (4, Barnett and Greenberg, 1969). And the economics of TV, where advertisers pay for head-count, made it inevitable that the relatively few commercial stations would all chase the mass audiences, that shortage of broadcast time would cause difficulties of fairness and equity and that various public policy objectives could not be well achieved (13, Greenberg and Barnett, 1971).

Then along came cable television with a very different supply curve for signal space. It does not use the atmosphere but a wire instead (3, Barnett and Greenberg, 1968; 2, Barnett, 1970). The present single coaxial cable with converters can now provide 20 to 26 channels. Similar dual cable systems double these figures, and with improved converters could provide 70 or so channels. There is no practical limit to channels available on wire (18, Sloan Commission, 1972; 10, Gabriel, 1968). Moreover, the average cost curve per channel declines monotonically.

Figure 5-1 illustrates the two supply curves for over-the-air broadcasting and cable broadcasting respectively in a community. The over-the-air supply curve rises because a UHF channel is more costly and less efficient than VHF. The curve becomes vertical when all frequency assignments are in use. The

*Perspectives on CATV Regulation* 81

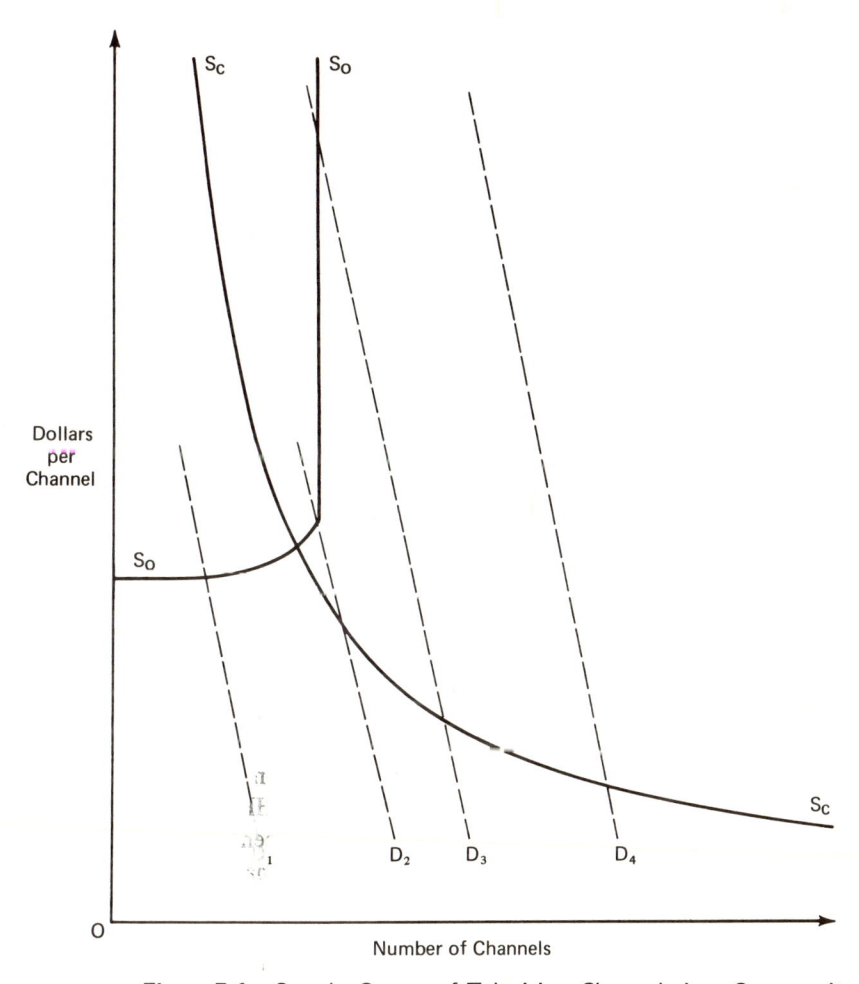

**Figure 5-1.** Supply Curves of Television Channels in a Community Over-the-air ($S_O$) and On Coaxial Cable ($S_C$)

cable cost curve reflects the inherent economies of scale of the coaxial wire. Where the over-the-air supply curve crosses the CATV differs among cities; cable cost depends upon the numbers of homes and the mileage of the wire network in each community.

The effect of increase in demand is quite different in the two alternative systems. In the over-the-air system, growth beyond $D_2$ generates large price increases and Ricardian rents (12, Greenberg, 1969; 1, Barnett, 1962). In the cable system such growth calls forth larger volumes of service at lower prices.

We can readily see the following. First, all the programs now excluded in over-the-air TV because of opportunity cost of foregone revenue from

## 82 Regulation in Further Perspective

mass audiences could be presented if they could but pay their own costs. Second, while cable is uneconomical if demand for channel capacity is small, the average cost per channel falls to extremely low levels if demand is large. Third, depending upon the extent to which demand grows through time, cable supply could become increasingly preferred.

The demand for channel supply *has* been shifting strongly to the right, in fact as well as in the above figure. The reasons are increasing affluence, high income elasticity of demand for entertainment, and innovations involving broadband communications services. Cable services have been becoming increasingly economical and desirable.

It would therefore appear that the FCC, in the light of public policy described earlier, should have welcomed with open arms the entrance of cable, which:

> overcomes the electromagnetic frequency limitation of over-the-air broadcasting;
> reduces oligopoly powers of networks and stations;
> fosters economical localism in various ways;
> could accommodate, as common carrier, very large numbers of independent suppliers;
> could liberate scarce over-the-air frequencies for other broadband services;
> has other virtues and uses.

### FCC Regulation of CATV to 1970

In view of these desirable characteristics of CATV in terms of free enterprise, competition, localism and scarce frequencies, what has been the actual FCC response to CATV?

The brief answer is that from the very beginning until recently the FCC devoted itself strenuously to eliminating CATV as a potentially significant supplier in television. It did so partly by simply proclaiming that this was in the public interest, and it did so partly by actions which denied CATV the opportunity to perform economic functions and gather rewards. It went beyond simply trying to protect the viability of over-the-air TV stations. It persistently sought to confine and subdue CATV to its original supplementary role as a community antenna in areas of poor signals.

Let us identify four additional significant functions of CATV in the performance of which it could achieve economic viability (4, Barnett and Greenberg, 1969). These are program imports, program origination, pay-TV and lease-TV, and new services:

> 1. CATV's entry and initial viability depend on signing on subscribers. This depends in the first instance upon importing outside signals for the subscribers.

2. Once having acquired sufficient subscribers to survive, CATV's opportunity is fruitfully to employ its extra channels in pursuit of further subscribers. This involves inexpensive program origination covering local events; public participation programs; automated and very low cost offerings such as weather, news, cartoons, stock market quotations, government and industry films; and, at a later date, when of suitable size and finances, more expensive programs.
3. Third, with a substantial subscriber list, CATV is then in an advantageous position to provide additional TV entertainment services: special sports and entertainment (pay-TV) and leased channels to entertainment suppliers (lease-TV).
4. Finally, CATV can then also use its extensive network and subscriber list to sell other services: meter reading; burglar alarm protection; specialized channels for use by health services, police and fire departments, education authorities, and other public bodies; specialized channel use for private organizations, such as shopping services and political programs; and eventually facsimile mail, library and data bank reference services, even computer tie-ins.

The FCC denied or greatly restrained the three CATV services which would compete with over-the-air broadcasting—program importation, program origination, and pay-TV and lease-TV—and thereby generally limited the economic viability and development of CATV. The following brief chronology gives evidence.

FCC's so-called Cox Report, prepared in *December, 1958* for the Senate Commerce Committee and for FCC publication by GPO, strongly indicted CATV thus: "A CATV system cannot cater to local preferences in programming, cannot serve local merchants, cannot provide a local news and weather service, cannot promote local civic and charitable enterprises, and cannot furnish a forum for discussion of local problems." (16 Phillips, 1972.)

In the *1962* Carter Mountain decision, the FCC denied common carrier facilities for CATV importation of TV programs, on the ground that the TV program offering would compete with and thus be economically harmful to a local TV station.

In a *1963* proposed rule and the subsequent *1965* First Report and Order, the FCC extended its restrictions on CATV program importation, and further required that programs shown by local stations not be duplicated on CATV.

In a *1966* Second Report and Order, the FCC strongly affirmed the policy that CATV (and pay-TV as well) may provide only supplementary service and must be subordinated to present and future over-the-air broadcasting. It imposed duplication protection of local stations. The FCC denied program imports into the top 100 TV markets, unless it was convincingly demonstrated to the FCC in evidentiary hearing in each individual case that ". . . such operation would be consistent with the public interest, and particularly the establishment and healthy maintenance of the UHF television broadcast service." Finally, the FCC proposed a bill to Congress to prohibit "cable casting"–program origination on CATV.

During the *1960s* the FCC approved language in Congressional copyright revision bills which would deny or greatly restrict CATV program imports into TV markets which were "adequately served," i.e., with 3 network signals.

In *December, 1968*, with further amendments in 1969, the FCC issued an extensive new proposed rule which did away with the evidentiary hearings of the 1966 order. It virtually prohibited program imports into the top 100 markets and limited the CATV firm's own program origination on the cable (other than on an automatic basis) to one channel, neither more nor less (21, FCC, 1968).

In *June, 1970* the FCC proposed to permit limited program imports by CATV but to require insertion of commercials supplied by local stations in place of the advertisements embodied in the imported programs.

It is obvious that the FCC persistently denied entrance and growth to cable TV in major markets, except as a local program antenna, by denying the provision of services which would sign on subscribers or otherwise yield revenue and economically justify the cable enterprises. Program imports and pay-TV were virtually prohibited and cable-casting limited. As a result, following the December, 1968 rule, cable industry growth in new systems and communities came to a halt.

### Why was the FCC Hostile?

The reasons given in FCC documents for trying to stifle CATV were that it was not free; it would bid away the best programs from free TV, and the poor would be deprived; it would displace over-the-air TV, and then rural areas would have no TV at all; and CATV program imports, having been found by the Courts to be legal and not to be copyright infringement, were unfair competition for over-the-air broadcasters, who had to pay for their programs. I have researched and written at length on these arguments elsewhere and will not repeat here, beyond saying they are in error or misleading (2, Barnett, 1970).

The real reasons for FCC obstruction of CATV development are much more interesting. The strongest is the FCC's identification with the over-the-air broadcasting industry, the industry with which the FCC's whole life has been intertwined, whose growth, splendors and achievements, have been the FCC's very own success. These are the industry and personnel with which the

FCC has lived closely every day, which it has fostered, protected, chastised, loved and occasionally hated, as closest kin. This is the industry with which professional broadcasting personnel have been interchanged—lawyers, engineers, clerks, commissioners—personnel who share a vested interest in the industry's professional specialization.

A second major reason for the effort by the FCC to stifle CATV is that the FCC's natural predilections were bolstered by strong political pressures from powerful groups: the broadcast industry, the movie industry, copyright interests, publishing-broadcast empires and allies in Congress.

A third reason, less obvious, is the FCC-sponsored All Channel Receiver Act (ACRA) which came into effect in 1964 and required that all TV receivers sold in the United States be capable of receiving UHF as well as VHF transmission. This continued the FCC's long-time efforts to bring large-scale UHF into active television supply. Based on FCC assurance that UHF development and the ACRA were necessary, Congress passed the legislation. The nation has now invested more than a billion dollars in UHF tuners on its sets, and is spending about $100 millions per year for the UHF tuners in new sets. If it should now turn out that cable and not UHF would have been a preferred path for TV expansion, then the FCC and its personnel made a costly error. No one likes to admit major errors, and government agencies less than most.

The final reason for the FCC's hostility to CATV was simply ignorance and unwillingness to learn.

In summary, until this year the FCC undertook to protect *its* industry from an invader. But how do we square FCC hostility to CATV with the fact that public policy in the basic statutes provides for competition, and CATV could greatly stimulate competition in television. The answer is that the FCC defined the relevant market to be *over-the-air broadcasting*. Within a market so defined, it does strive for competition—witness its efforts to limit network power, to encourage FM and UHF, to limit the number of stations which may be owned by one company. What the FCC could not accept was a startling and intolerable idea: that competitive forces unforeseen by it, outside its definition of the market, which it had at first ignored and later obstructed, would make much of its past behavior appear foolish and its future presence perhaps unnecessary.

### Enter New Forces

In 1969 a new game began, not intended and indeed unforeseen by the FCC. The limited hearings on the December, 1968 notice of inquiry and proposed rule-making which the FCC had contemplated, got out of hand. A storm of protest arose, and a great deal of new material and commentary came to light. As a result, Congressional hearings were then conducted in the House of Representatives, at which there was substantial testimony in opposition to the proposed FCC rule making (20, United States Congress, 1969). Congressional pressure was put on the White House to release the Report of the President's Task Force on Communications Policy to Congress and the public (23, United States President's Task Force, 1968). It was found to favor expansion of CATV, and otherwise to be in opposition to FCC proposals. The Task Force Chairman, Undersecretary of State Eugene Rostow, in a speech to the American Management Association stated "that the FCC's actions in the Notice were inconsistent with its professed goals and that it had 'ordered what is for all practical purposes a standstill in the industry for an indefinite period.' " (6, Broadcasting, 1969.) The prestigious Sloan Commission on Cable Communications conducted a half-million dollar inquiry on the cable innovation and released a public report favorable to CATV in 1971 (18, Sloan Commission, 1971).

Further, there was change in the FCC. The testimony and public controversy apparently influenced the views of several commissioners, notably Nicholas Johnson and perhaps Rex Lee, who were not hostile to CATV nor committed to defending past FCC decisions concerning UHF. And the membership of the FCC began to change following the entrance of the new administration. Among those who departed were Commissioners Rosel Hyde (chairman) and Kenneth Cox, who had been strongly identified with doctrines of protecting over-the-air broadcasting and efforts to render CATV non-viable.

A new Commissioner became Chairman of the FCC and a new Director was appointed to head the Office of Telecommunications Policy in the White House. Neither had obligations to past FCC decisions or to over-the-air broadcasting or to CATV. Both, it became apparent, committed themselves to politically acceptable, compromise solutions of the CATV hassle.

It took longer than they expected; but finally, in February and July, 1972, the FCC gave birth to an enormous document, formulated by and acceptable to the broadcasting industry, the cable industry, the Administration, and a majority of the FCC. It has been issued as a final Cable Television Report and Order (22, FCC 1972).

### FCC Regulation, 1972

The most important fact in the new regulations is that CATV firms will be permitted to enter and develop in major metropolitan areas. They will import, originate multiple programs, and provide multiple channels. In the top 100 markets, which reaches all the way down, for example, to Lansing, Michigan, Madison, Wisconsin, and Columbia, South Carolina, two commercial stations may be imported, and educational television and foreign language stations may be imported in addition. In all television markets, cable-casting by the CATV firm and others is required on multiple channels and is permitted on further channels. Clearly the FCC has reversed the views it held when the proposed rule-making three years earlier effectively denied all imports, limited the CATV firm's cablecasting to one channel, and denied other revenue sources. The FCC accepts the fact of significant promise in cable service and no longer desires to freeze the CATV industry at its present level.

The second most important fact is that the FCC has not at all given up its rather strong identification with over-the-air broadcasting stations and networks. It remains intensely concerned that the VHF and networks should continue to flourish and that UHF should grow in audience revenues and viability. In numerous ways it has fenced in CATV where cable might have adverse impact on over-the-air broadcasters, and it has erected protective walls around over-the-air broadcasting and its revenue sources. In its own words,

> The rationale for permitting at least two additional signals in all major markets is simply this: It appears that two signals not available in the community is the minimum amount of new service needed to attract large amounts of investment capital for the construction of new systems and to open the way for the full development of cable's potential. We will, therefore, permit this complement of signals in the larger markets because it is necessary in terms of cable's requirements and because it is acceptable in terms of impact on broadcasting (22, FCC 1972).

To protect over-the-air broadcasting and restrain CATV, the FCC has done all of the following:

> limited CATV imports of commercial station signals to two in the 100 largest markets; and in smaller markets which are served by three networks and one independent station, denied commercial station imports altogether;
> required that the two imported signals, where authorized, be from nearby cities, rather than leading stations from New York, Los Angeles, Chicago, or elsewhere;
> imposed program exclusivity protection for local stations, whereby CATV may not duplicate local station programs for a year or two, and must blackout such programs on imported signals;
> imposed strong blackout restrictions on CATV importation or carriage of sports programs;
> denied carriage by CATV of the signals which can, in fact, be received over-the-air from nearby "overlapping" markets;
> emasculated cable pay TV by prohibiting programs which TV stations or networks usually buy. Thus FCC denies to cable pay-TV the showing of films between 2 and 10 years old; sports programs which are less than 2 years old; or any series programs with interconnected plots or using the same cast of principal characters. And it further constrains pay-TV by not permitting revenue advertisements before or after, as well as during programs;
> required concurrence by the local ETV station and educational

*88 Regulation in Further Perspective*

authorities before permitting importation of outside ETV signals; recommended and endorsed provisions for the new copyright statutes which greatly extend protection of stations, networks and copyright.

A third important attribute of the new FCC policy is an unusual emphasis on experimentation, learning, and flexibility, at least during the early stages of the innovation and its diffusion. "Cable television is an emerging technology that promises a communications revolution. Inevitably our regulatory pattern must evolve as cable evolves—and no one can say what the precise dimensions will be." Regrettably, however, there is nowhere the slightest hint that perhaps Federal regulation of cable TV should disappear or be greatly reduced, or should not have begun.

**Multiple Government Regulation**

Finally, a fourth important element in the new national policy concerns the levels of government which will be involved in TV regulation. The FCC could have entirely preempted CATV regulation. The National Cable Television Association (NCTA) and other cable interests urged that it do so, so that they might escape franchise regulation and possible public utility regulation. CATV would greatly prefer to join the FCC family and enjoy something like the beneficent monopoly protections, license and profits which the FCC has characteristically provided for over-the-air broadcasters. For example, the NCTA testified that "... no rate regulations of any kind are needed" (22, FCC 1972). Broadcasters generally preferred multiple government regulation for CATV, as did state and local governments because of their vested and bureaucratic interests.

The FCC declined to preempt entirely regulation of CATV and opted for what it calls dual jurisdiction. The FCC sets the rules for CATV firms and standards and guidelines for franchises and local regulation. Local governments grant the franchises and engage in a significant degree of cable system supervision. The FCC general rules:

require carriage of local stations;
restrict program imports;
impose sports and station duplication blackouts;
require dedicated, free channels for public access, education, and government, and other channels for self-origination and lease;
utilize the FCC's "fairness" doctrine for CATV;
require at least 20 channels initially, expansion when needed, and a rudimentary two-way capacity;
impose technical standards;
prohibit joint ownership of TV and CATV properties

The franchise and local regulation standards which must be followed include:

> public proceedings in franchise awards;
> awards for 15 years or less;
> construction progress;
> franchise fee limits of three to five percent;
> complaint procedures;
> supervised rates.

A separate role for state governments is not defined, but presumably they may preempt the local government role and/or impose those aspects of public utility or other regulation which are not inconsistent with FCC rules. Nothing in the FCC order disturbs current or future state regulation, which has been slowly occurring. Connecticut, Nevada, Rhode Island, Vermont, and Puerto Rico regulate through the state PUC. New York, Massachusetts, and Hawaii have statewide regulation, but not by PUC. Litigation is under way in Illinois.

### Concluding Comments

My first comment is regret over loss of "what could have been." CATV was a first step toward the wired city (Barnett and Greenberg 1968-71; 19, Smith, 1970). The only regulation necessary was to require that the CATV firm be a common carrier open to all at reasonable rates, as are telephone companies. With common carrier operation and capacity expanded as demand required, there was no need to regulate what would be sent on the wire or by whom, any more than it is necessary to regulate newspapers, mimeograph machines, movies, sports, advertisements, concert halls, auditoriums or printing presses. Cable video, audio and other services would have developed as they were useful, efficient, and economical, at constant or declining costs, as in the case of telephone and other wire services. The opportunities and prospects were exciting (18, Sloan Commission, 1971; Barnett and Greenberg references, 1968-1971; 8, Dardick, et al., 1969; 9, E.I.A., 1969; 11, Goldmark, 1970; 24, White, 1968).

The second comment is also regret, at the grotesque busyness and complexity of the FCC regulations. Here is a caricature of the bumbling official trying to manage and direct all the details of growth and change of a little understood innovation which promises to be a seed bed for further innovations. Here is interference in a super degree by a bureaucracy of demonstrably poor record in an Administration with demonstrably little respect for the First Amendment, egged on by powerful, vested business interests which are trying to keep existing monopolies and suppress would-be competition.

My final comment is pleasure that cable television and other services will probably, in fact, develop strongly during the next generation or so. It will be at a slower pace, more clumsily, inefficiently, and with hazards. But, hopefully, a great innovation is nevertheless on the way.

## REFERENCES TO CHAPTER FIVE

Barnett, H.J. *Economics of Television Markets.* St. Louis: Washington University mimeo. 1964. Filed with Federal Communications Commission 32 FCC 811 (Docket 14223, 1962).

Barnett, H.J. *Resistance to the Wires City.* St. Louis: Washington University, mimeo, 1970. Reprinted in *Spatial, Regional, and Population Economics,* ed. M. Perlman. London: Gordon and Breach, forthcoming, 1973.

Barnett, H.J. and Greenberg, E. *A Proposal for Wired City Television,* P-3668, Santa Monica, Calif.: RAND Corp., 1967. Subsequently published in *Washington University Law Quarterly,* Winter 1968, pp. 1-25, and reprinted in *The Radio Spectrum.* Washington, D.C.: Brookings Institution, 1968. Condensed version in *American Economic Review,* June 1968, 58.

Barnett, H.J. and Greenberg, E. "Regulating CATV Systems," *Law and Contemporary Problems,* 1969, 34, pp. 562-585.

Briggs, A. *The Birth of Broadcasting.* London: Oxford University Press, 1961; *The Golden Age of Wireless,* London: Oxford University Press, 1965. (V. 1 and 2, of the *History of Broadcasting in the U.K.*)

*Broadcasting Magazine,* March 17, 1969, p. 146.

Coase, R. *British Broadcasting, A Study in Monopoly.* Cambridge: Harvard University Press, 1950.

Dordick, H., Chesler, L., Firstman, S., and Bretz, R. *Telecommunications in Urban Development.* RM-6069-RC. Santa Monica, Calif.: RAND Corporation, 1969.

Electronic Industries Association (EIA), *The Future of Broadband Communications.* Washington, D.C.: EIA, 2001 Eye St., N.W. Submitted to the Federal Communications Commission, Docket 18397, October 27, 1969.

Gabriel, R.P. "A Comparison of Wired and Wireless Broadcasting for the Future," *Royal Television Society Journal,* 1968, 12.

Goldmark, Peter. *Broadcasting Magazine,* Dec. 21, 1970, 79, p. 32.

Greenberg, E. "Television Station Profitability and FCC Regulating Policy," *Journal of Industrial Economics,* July 1969.

Greenberg, E. and Barnett, H.J. "Program Diversity—New Evidence and Old Theories," *American Economic Review,* May 1971, 61.

Jones, W. *Regulated Industries.* Brooklyn: The Foundation Press, 1967.

Paulu, B. *Radio and TV Broadcasting on the European Continent.* Minneapolis: University of Minnesota Press, 1967.

Phillips, M. *CATV,* Evanston, Ill.: Northwestern University Press, 1972. Ms. Phillips quotes from U.S. FCC, *The Television Inquiry: The Problem of Television Service for Smaller Communities,* prepared for the Committee on Interstate and Foreign Commerce, Hearings on S. 224 and S. 376, 85th Congress, 2nd session, 1958, pp. 3834-47.

Schildhause, Sol. Address before Section of Public Utility Law, American Bar Association, August 12, 1969; quoted by C.O. Verrill, Jr. *Law and Contemporary Problems,* Summer 1969, 34, p. 606.

Sloan Commission on Communications. *On the Cable.* New York: McGraw-Hill, 1972.

Smith, R. "The Wired Nation," *The Nation*, May 18, 1970, *210*.

United States Congress, House of Representatives. Hearings Before the Committee on Interstate and Foreign Commerce, 91st Congress, 1st Session (May 19-23, 1969).

United States Federal Communications Commission, Docket No. 18397, Relative to CATV, Washington, D.C., December 12, 1968. Various FCC documents and hearings.

United States Federal Communications Commission. *Cable Television Report and Order,* February 3, 1972; *Cable Television Service Reconsideration of Report and Order,* July 14, 1972. Washington, D.C.: FCC.

United States President's Task Force on Communications Policy, *Final Report.* Chapter 7, Washington, D.C.: U.S. Government Printing Office, 1968.

White, Stephen, "Toward a Modest Experiment in Cable Television," *The Public Interest*, Summer 1968, pp. 52-66.

Chapter Six

# Reversals in Peak and Offpeak Prices

Elizabeth E. Bailey and Lawrence J. White

## I. Introduction

Can it be rational for the supplier of a monopoly service, such as transportation or public utilities, to charge a price during peak periods that is *lower* than the price in off-peak periods? Such a pricing possibility has been virtually ignored in economists' discussions of peak-load pricing. Yet, such pricing structures sometimes are found in practice. For instance, the daily peak in an electric utility is often generated mainly by business customers who pay less for service than residential customers whose evening demand is off-peak.*

Most theoretical treatments of peak-load pricing reach the conclusion that peak prices will be higher than off-peak prices. This result follows automatically in the standard model in which there is a welfare objective and the firm has constant returns to scale in production. We show that a higher peak price also occurs in a model in which the firm can levy a perfect two-part tariff.

What has not been recognized is that a peak price less than the offpeak price *can be optimal* in other models of firm behavior. Specifically, reversals can occur when:

(i) the firm has a welfare objective, but there are decreasing average costs in production, so that a profit constraint is explicitly or implicitly imposed;

---

*We are particularly grateful to Paul W. MacAvoy, William J. Baumol, Gerald R. Faulhaber and Edward E. Zajac, each of whom made substantial contributions to the paper. Our thanks also go to a number of other colleagues in the Bell System and in the academic community who were of help to us. Part of this research was conducted while Lawrence White held a post-doctoral fellowship in Public Utility Economics from the American Telephone and Telegraph Company. The views expressed in the paper are those of the authors, and should not be interpreted as reflecting official opinion or policy of Bell Laboratories or of the American Telephone and Telegraph Company. Reprinted from the *Bell Journal of Economics and Management Science*, Spring 1974.

(ii) the firm has a profit rather than a welfare objective, and faces a demand in the off-peak period that is sufficiently more *inelastic* than that during the peak so as to compensate at the margin for the attribution of capacity costs to the peak period;
(iii) the firm is subject to a rate-of-return constraint, which gives it an incentive to lower the rate to the peak users while keeping the off-peak rate at the monopoly level; and
(iv) the firm employs a multi-part pricing scheme, but one that is imperfect in extracting all the consumer's surplus.

Such models do not exhaust the situations that can lead to pricing reversals, but they do suggest that there are a number of important cases in which such reversals can be explained by rational economic processes.

The models are also important in a second respect, for in some of them, we are able to demonstrate that capacity may be expanded beyond the level that maximizes welfare. In particular, rate-of-return regulation can lead to such overexpansion of capacity, and may do so whether a single or a multi-part tariff is levied.

## II. The Profit Versus the Welfare Objective

**Welfare Maximization.** Virtually all of the literature dealing with peak-load pricing principles seeks to determine the conditions necessary for maximization of social welfare in the sense of Pareto optimality or of maximization of consumer's plus producers' surplus.[1] We will begin by reviewing the results obtained with a simple version of this model.

Our presentation assumes that there are two periods of equal duration and that demands in the two periods are not related. To make this seem sensible, think of the model as depicting two classes of customers, such as business users of power and residential users, whose demand for the facilities occurs during the day and evening, respectively.[2] The cost structure consists of a constant operating expense per unit of demand served, and a constant cost per unit of capacity. We shall suppose that the outcome in terms of capacity usage is that there is a distinct period of peak and a period of off-peak (rather than that there is a joint peak). These simplifying assumptions are made so that we can focus directly on the pricing reversal phenomenon, and so that straightforward graphical interpretations can be presented. The consequences of relaxing some of the assumptions are discussed later in the paper.

The mathematical formulation portrays the maximization of the sum of producer's and consumers' surplus, given by the integrals of demand curves less costs, as summarized by Model (1) in Table 6-1, where $\overline{X}$ and $\underline{X}$ are demands in the peak ($\overline{X}$) and off-peak ($\underline{X}$) periods, respectively, with peak period demand equaling capacity, $\overline{p}$ and $\underline{p}$ are prices in the peak ($\overline{p}$) and off-peak ($\underline{p}$) periods, respectively, $c$ is the operating expense per unit of output (constant), $\overline{k}$

is the acquisition cost per unit of capacity (constant), $r$ is the market cost of capital (constant), and the subscript $W$ denotes values relating to the welfare-maximization objective.

Equations (2) and (3) indicate that peak price covers both the expense cost generated by the peak traffic and the marginal capacity cost, whereas off-peak price just covers its own expense cost. It is immediately obvious from (2) and (3) that

$$\overline{p}_W > \underline{p}_W$$

so that *if there are constant costs, welfare maximization automatically requires the peak price to be higher than the off-peak price.* The familiar pricing rule has appeared.

The results are made clearer by Steiner's (1957) peak-load geometry as displayed in Figure 6-1. Equation (2) is just satisfied at point $\overline{W}$. Equation (3) is satisfied at $\underline{W}$. Since price is equated with the relevant costs in each case, and since costs are constant, the firm just exactly breaks even by supplying capacity $X = \overline{X}_W$ and total demand $D = \overline{X}_W + \underline{X}_W$ at prices $\overline{p}_W$ and $\underline{p}_W$ respectively.

**Profit Maximization.** Now let us contrast these results with those that follow when the firm's objective is to maximize profit rather than producer's plus consumers' surplus. The relevant model is (4) in Table 6-1, where the subscript M is used to denote values relating to the profit objective of the monopoly firm. The $\overline{e}$ and $\underline{e}$ are price elasticities of demand in the peak and off-peak periods, respectively.

When elasticities are equal, (5) and (6) show that peak and off-peak prices are in the same ratio as the marginal costs of peak and off-peak service, and thus off-peak price in this case will always be lower than peak price. However, off-peak rates are *higher* than peak rates whenever

$$c \left[ \frac{1}{1 - \frac{1}{\underline{e}}} \right] > (c + rk) \left[ \frac{1}{1 - \frac{1}{\overline{e}}} \right].$$

Thus, *off-peak price can be higher than peak price if off-peak service has demand that is sufficiently more inelastic than the peak service so as to compensate for the larger marginal costs attributable to the peak service. It is clear that the size of* rk *relative to* c *is also important in the determination of pricing reversals. If marginal capacity costs are large relative to marginal operating expenses, then the pricing reversal is less likely to occur.*

In terms of the electricity example, the pricing reversal may occur if rate schedules are "a result of pricing policies based on value of service."[3] Residential users place a higher value on such service, i.e., have a more inelastic de-

## Table 6-1. Summary of Results

| Model | Peak Price | Offpeak Price |
|---|---|---|
| *Welfare Maximization* (1) | (2) | (3) |
| $\underset{\overline{X},\underline{X}}{\text{Maximize}} \ W = \int_0^{\overline{X}} \overline{p} \, d\overline{X} + \int_0^{\underline{X}} \underline{p} \, d\underline{X} - c(\overline{X}+\underline{X}) - rk\overline{X}$ | $\overline{p}_W = c + rk$ | $\underline{p}_W = c$ |
| *Profit Maximization* (4) | (5) | (6) |
| $\underset{\overline{X},\underline{X}}{\text{Maximize}} \ \pi = \overline{p}(\overline{X})\overline{X} + \underline{p}(\underline{X})\underline{X} - c(\overline{X}+\underline{X}) - rk\overline{X}$ | $\overline{p}_M = \dfrac{c+rk}{1 - \dfrac{1}{\overline{e}}}$ | $\underline{p}_M = \dfrac{c}{1 - \dfrac{1}{\underline{e}}}$ |
| *Increasing Returns in Capacity Provision* (7) | (8) | (9) |
| $\underset{\overline{X},\underline{X}}{\text{Maximize}} \ W = \int_0^{\overline{X}} \overline{p} \, d\overline{X} + \int_0^{\underline{X}} \underline{p} \, d\underline{X} - c(\overline{X}+\underline{X}) - K(\overline{X})$ <br> subject to $\overline{p}(\overline{X})\overline{X} + \underline{p}(\underline{X})\underline{X} - c(\overline{X}+\underline{X}) - K(\overline{X}) \geq 0$ | $\overline{p}_I = \dfrac{(1+\lambda)(c+K')}{1+\lambda\left(1-\dfrac{1}{\overline{e}}\right)}$ | $\underline{p}_I = \dfrac{(1+\lambda)c}{1+\lambda\left(1-\dfrac{1}{\underline{e}}\right)}$ |

## Reversals in Peak and Offpeak Prices

| | (10) | (11) | (12) |
|---|---|---|---|
| *Rate-of-Return Regulation* <br><br> Maximize $\pi = p(\overline{X})\overline{X} + p(\underline{X})\underline{X} - c(\overline{X}+\underline{X}) - rk(\overline{X}+Z)$ <br> $\overline{X}, \underline{X}, Z$ <br><br> subject to $p(\overline{X})\overline{X} + p(\underline{X})\underline{X} - c(\overline{X}+\underline{X}) - sk(\overline{X}+Z) \leq 0$ | | $\overline{p}_G = \dfrac{c + rk - \dfrac{\lambda}{1-\lambda}(s-r)k}{1 - \dfrac{1}{e}}$ | $\underline{p}_G = \dfrac{1}{1-\dfrac{1}{e}}$ |
| | | (23) | (24) |
| *Perfect Two-Part Tariff* <br><br> See Text | | $\overline{p}_T = c + rk$ | $\underline{p}_T = c$ |
| | | (25) | (26) |
| *Regulation of Rate of Return but not of Price Structure* <br><br> See Text | | $\overline{p}_R = c + rk - \dfrac{\lambda}{1-\lambda}(s-r)z$ | $\underline{p}_R = c$ |

## 98 Regulation in Further Perspective

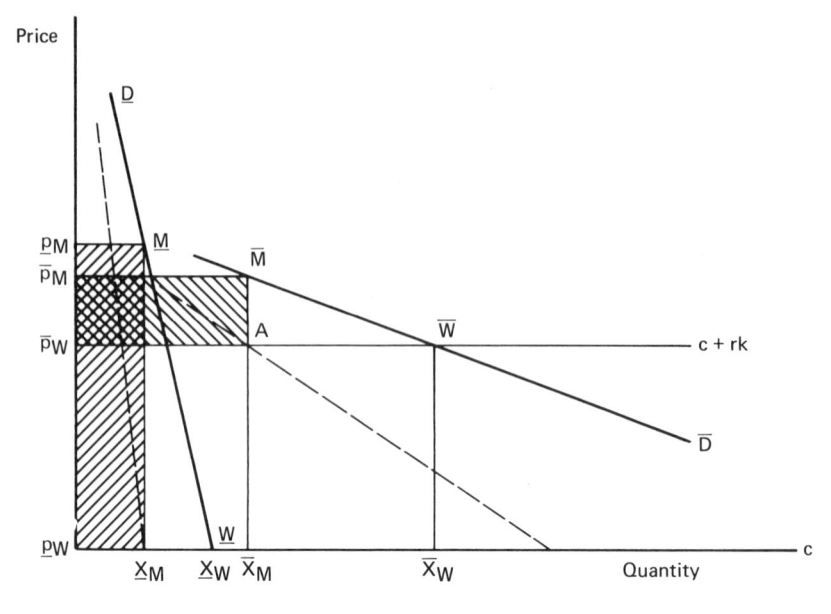

**Figure 6-1.** Welfare Versus Monopoly Pricing

mand, than do the business users since large business customers are more likely to be able to generate their own electricity or to convert to alternative sources of energy.

The monopoly solution is described graphically in Figure 6-1. Equations (5) and (6) are satisfied at points $\overline{M}$ and $\underline{M}$ respectively, with $\underline{p}_M > \overline{p}_M$ so that the off-peak price is higher and the reversal occurs. Profits are given by the sum of the two striped rectangles $p_M MB p_W$ and $\overline{p}_M \overline{MA} \overline{p}_W$, with the height of the former rectangle being given by the difference between off-peak price and operating expense, and the height of the latter rectangle being given by the difference between peak price and the sum of operating and capacity expense. Notice, however, that it is not correct to refer to rectangle $p_M MB p_W$ as "off-peak profit" and $\overline{p}_M \overline{MA} \overline{p}_W$ as "peak profit". Since peak and off-peak users share some common capacity, any attribution of costs and profits runs into the familiar joint-cost problem.

**Welfare Maximization with Increasing Returns in Capacity Provision.** Most firms for which the peak-load pricing problem is relevant have increasing returns to scale in the provision of capacity,[4] that is, capacity costs are given by $K(\overline{X})$, $K' > 0$, $K'' < 0$. Figure 6-2 illustrates the situation. At the output pair $(\underline{W}, \overline{W})$ where welfare is maximized, price equals marginal cost for each user, $\underline{p}_W = c$ and $\overline{p}_W = c + K'$. Under such a scheme the firm operates at a loss whose magnitude is given by the dotted area $B\overline{W}\overline{p}_W$. If a single price is all

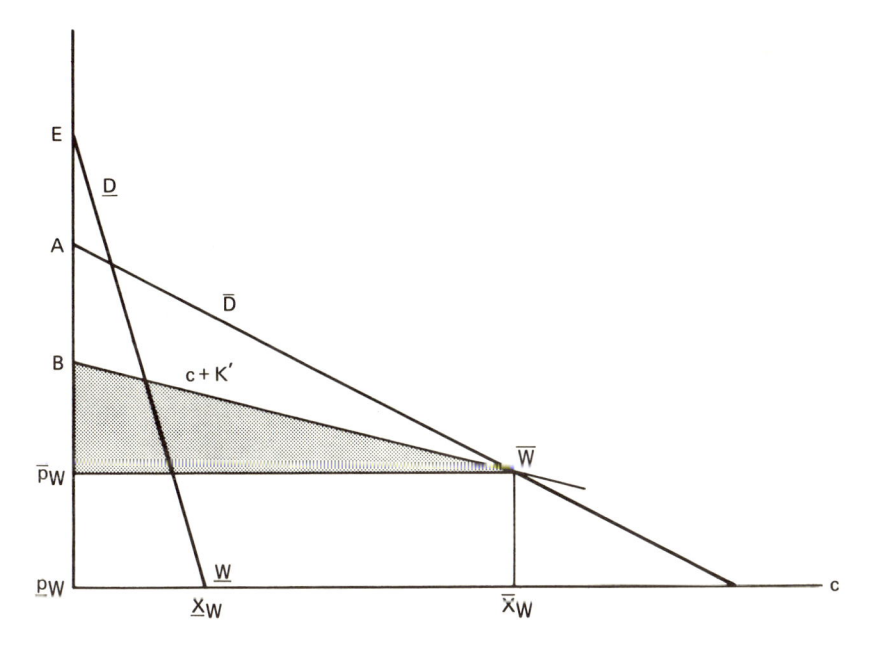

[Figure 6-2 depicts axes with labels E, A, B, $\bar{p}_W$, $\underline{p}_W$ on the vertical axis; $\underline{x}_W$, $\bar{x}_W$, c on the horizontal axis; lines labeled $\underline{D}$, $\bar{D}$, $c+K'$, $\underline{W}$, $\bar{W}$.]

**Figure 6-2.** Increasing Returns to Capacity

that can be levied for each type of customer, and if the firm is to break even in its operations, the appropriate model is given by (7) in Table 6-1.

The pricing rules (8) and (9) can be interpreted as stating that the deviation of price from marginal cost for each period should be proportional to the marginal deficit incurred by the last unit of output in that period.[5] It is clear that we can obtain from (8) and (9) an equation that indicates the conditions under which the pricing reversal $\underline{p}_I > \bar{p}_I$ occurs just as we did previously. Furthermore, precisely the same qualitative statements about elasticities hold in the breakeven welfare-maximization model as held in the profit maximization model.

### III. The Regulated Firm

**Breakeven Regulation.** We now consider a peak-load pricing model with profit maximization as the objective but with a regulatory constraint on the firm's behavior. If the constraint binds the firm in such a way that its total revenue just covers its total cost, including the cost of capital, then no unique solution to the peak-load pricing problem exists. With the profit goal, any pair of peak and off-peak prices consistent with the zero-profit constraint is equally desirable to management.

**Rate-of-Return Regulation.** If the Averch-Johnson [1962] assumption of a fair return, $s$, larger than the market cost of capital, $r$, is made, then a unique pair of peak and off-peak prices can be attained. Model (10) in Table 6-1 follows Bailey [1972] but uses the idea from Bailey [1973] that operation off the production frontier is a possible alternative for the firm.[6] We use $d$ to denote the multiplier associated with the rate-of-return constraint, $Z$ for the number of units of capital wasted, and the subscript $G$ to denote the solution prices for the model.

Equations (11) and (12) give the rules for peak and off-peak prices. Equation (12) is precisely the same as the rule followed by the unregulated profit-maximizing firm, c.f., Equation (12) and Equation (6). Thus, in the absence of cross-elasticity effects, (12) says that the off-peak quantity and price are identical to that which an unregulated monopoly would attain; the constraint does not affect the off-peak policy.[7]

The entire effect of regulation is reflected instead in peak price changes and/or in the possibility of operating off the production frontier. Equation (11) gives the peak-period effect. Marginal revenue is set equal to something less than the marginal cost in the peak period. Intuitively, because constrained profits increase with the level of capacity, the firm passes on the benefits of regulation to those users whose increased demand will cause an increase in capacity. *Thus, the peak period price under rate-of-return regulation will be lower than the peak period price in a model of unconstrained profit maximization, c.f., (11) and (5). Accordingly, the likelihood is increased of finding the pricing reversal described in Section II.*

This model also has some interesting implications as to the capacity that is provided.[8] Let us denote the surplus of off-peak revenues over off-peak operating costs as

$$\underline{S} = \underline{p}\underline{X} - c\underline{X},$$

and let us assume for the moment that the firm operates on the production frontier ($Z_G = 0$). Then the constraint in model (11) can be rewritten

$$\underline{S} + \overline{p}_G \overline{X}_G - c\overline{X}_G - rk\overline{X}_G = (s-r)k\overline{X}_G,$$

which can be used to determine the conditions under which the peak-period capacity of the regulated monopoly would exceed or fall short of the socially optimal level of capacity.

This equation tells us that once the surplus from the off-peak period has been determined, the firm portrayed by this model would choose the peak-period quantity (= capacity) and price to bring its *overall* profits in line with the constraint. In choosing its peak-period capacity, the firm would thereby determine its rate base and the level of allowable profits under the constraint. The surplus from the off-peak period (already determined) and the surplus or deficits from the peak period (equal to peak revenues minus the sum of peak operating costs and total capacity costs) must together sum to the total allowable profits under the constraint.[9]

More specifically, if the off-peak surplus is very large, the firm would lower its peak price below $c + rk$, and thus run a deficit on its peak period operations. It would do this in order to absorb its off-peak surplus and at the same time to expand its capacity and thus expand its allowable profits. The firm would continue to lower its price and expand its capacity until the allowable profits on the expanded rate base equal the off-peak surplus less the peak period deficit. The rate-of-return constraint has given the firm an incentive to absorb its extra profits through expanded peak capacity rather than changing its off-peak price to reduce profits. If, on the other hand, the off-peak surplus is comparatively small, the firm will raise its peak price and make a surplus on its peak operations, until the sum of the off-peak and peak surplus comes into equality with the allowable profits (which are being reduced because the higher price causes a reduction in capacity).

These last results expand considerably on one of Bailey's principal conclusions. Bailey shows [1972, p 676] that the peak period capacity may exceed the welfare maximization level if cross-elasticity is not zero. Here, we see a more general result: *Peak period capacity exceeds the welfare maximization level whenever the surplus from the off-peak period is large enough to require deficits in the peak period.*[10] *In the other case, in which there is some surplus in the peak period, the regulated firm will provide a larger capacity than would an unregulated monopolist, $\overline{X}_M < \overline{X}_G$, but below that which welfare maximization produces, $\overline{X}_G < \overline{X}_W$.* The crucial variables determining whether or not the peak capacity exceeds the the welfare maximizing level are the size of the off-peak surplus and the *margin* between $s$ and $r$. As the margin between $s$ and $r$ is reduced, the constrained level of profits declines, and it becomes more likely that the off-peak surplus will have to be absorbed by an expansion of peak period capacity and consequent peak period deficits. Note, though, that if the margin between $s$ and $r$ narrows because $s$ is lowered, peak-period capacity will expand; whereas, if the margin narrows because $r$ rises, the peak-period capacity will not change but the welfare maximizing capacity level will decline. These last results follow from the constraint in model (10), in which $s$, but not $r$, is a determinant of the peak-period capacity.[11]

We now examine the possibility of $Z > 0$, i.e., the possibility that the firm is operating off its production frontier by employing excess capital. If $Z > 0$, then the Kuhn-Tucker condition on the variable $Z$ requires that $\lambda = \frac{r}{s}$.[12] Substituting into (11), we can see that this happens only when

$$\overline{p} = \frac{c}{1 - \frac{1}{e}}$$

## 102  Regulation in Further Perspective

The common sense of this equation is straightforward. The firm wishes to expand its capacity to absorb its off-peak surplus. If it is worthwhile to expand capacity at the point where the marginal revenue equals marginal operating cost, then the best way of expanding capital further is to add capital that is not used productively. Such an addition of unproductive capital does not necessitate any price drop, whereas adding productive capacity means that the price and marginal revenue on peak operation has to drop and the firm's marginal expenditure on operating costs exceeds the additional revenue it brings in.[13] For the rest of this section, we shall suppose that $MR_G > c$ at the optimal solution, so that the operation off the production frontier is not a profitable alternative.

The results under rate-of-return regulation may be seen graphically in Figure 6-3. As before, the profit-maximizer's solution is denoted $\bar{M}$ and $\underline{M}$, and the welfare solution is $\bar{W}$ and $\underline{W}$. The horizontal line $c + sk$ is constructed so that the difference between it and the $c + rk$ line is precisely the permitted return $(s - r)k$ per unit of capacity.

For the regulated firm, constrained profits at any given peak period output $X_G$ (= capacity) would be equal to $(s - r)kX_G$, or the solid rectangle $\bar{p}_W BFE$. If, as in the diagram, the surplus from the off-peak period, the striped rectangle $\underline{p}_G GH \underline{p}_W$, exceeds $\bar{p}_W BFE$, the firm would set a price $\bar{p}_G$ for the peak period that was below $c + rk$ until the deficits, dotted rectangle $\bar{p}_W EG \bar{p}_G$, were such that $\underline{p}_G GH\underline{p}_W - \bar{p}_W EG\bar{p}_G = \bar{p}_W BFE$. This last condition can also be restated as $\underline{p}_G GH\underline{p}_W = \bar{p}_W BFE + \bar{p}_W EG\bar{p}_G$ or $\underline{p}_G GH\underline{p}_W = BF\bar{G}\bar{p}_G$, i.e., the striped rectangle is equal to the sum of the solid and dotted rectangles in Figure 6-3. In effect, then, the regulated firm finds that point on its peak demand curve $\bar{G}$ at

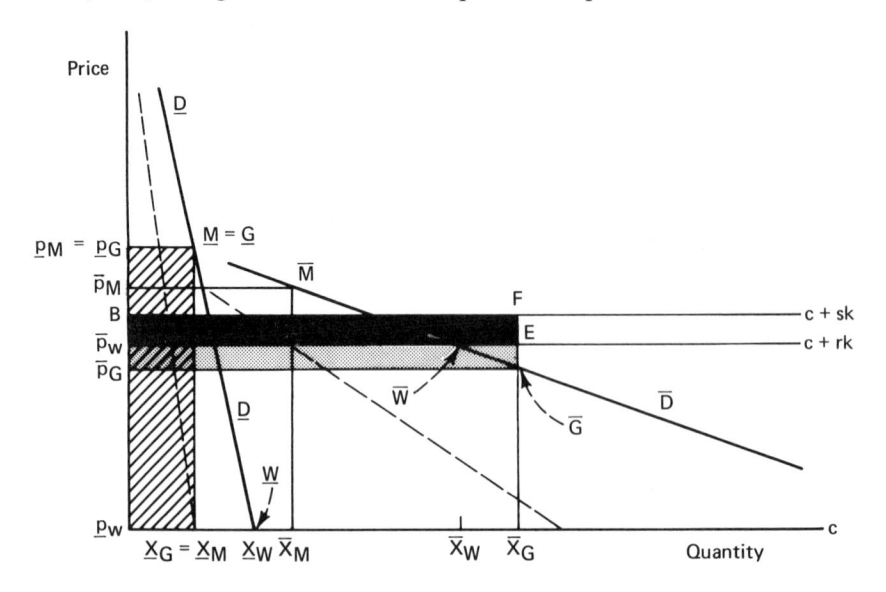

**Figure 6-3.** Pricing Under Rate-of-Return Regulation

which the product of the *margin* between $c + sk$ and $\overline{p}_G$, times the $\overline{X}_G$ that is forthcoming at that $\overline{p}_G$, is just equal to the off-peak surplus. This result has a simple interpretation in common sense terms: $c + sk$ represents the maximum that the firm could charge for peak sales if it had no off-peak surplus. But if the firm has an off-peak surplus, it cannot charge the full $c + sk$ for its peak operations. Hence, it drops its peak price until the difference between $c + sk$ and its peak price, times the peak quantity, can just absorb the off-peak surplus.

As is clear from the diagram, if the margin $(s - r)k$ (the distance $FE$) is smaller than the distance $F\overline{G}$, the firm will be running a deficit in the peak period and the regulated firm will be providing peak capacity that is larger than that which maximizes welfare. The opposite will be true if the distance $FE$ is larger than the distance $F\overline{G}$. Note, though, as was argued before, if $r$ moves relative to $s$, the peak capacity offered does not change (though the welfare maximizing level changes). Thus, in the diagram, if $r$ increases so that the margin $(s - r)k$ is diminished, the peak output $\overline{X}_G$ does not change. This is true because $\overline{X}_G$ is still the only point at which $BF\overline{G}p_G = \underline{p}_G GH p_W$. All that is implied is that the firm is running larger losses on its unchanged peak output and its overall profits are reduced. If, on the other hand, $s$ declines $BF\overline{G}p_G$ is no longer equal to $\underline{p}_G GH p_W$, and $\overline{X}_G$ has to increase.

### IV. Two-Part Tariffs

**Perfect Two-Part Tariff.** The preceding sections have described models in which only one charge is levied on peak users and one on off-peak users. In practice, however, firms such as public utilities usually have a set of multiple prices or block tariffs with prices falling in steps as greater volumes are used. To reflect such a system of prices, we now introduce a model of peak-load pricing in which a customer charge as well as a usage charge is levied.

To avoid complicating the model, we suppose that the firm can charge an entrance fee or customer charge to each class of customers, as well as a peak and an off-peak usage price. Furthermore, we assume that all customers in a particular customer class have identical demand curves.[14]

If the firm has complete freedom in setting the customer fees, $\overline{E}$ and $\underline{E}$, and the usage fees, $\overline{p}$ and $\underline{p}$, the model becomes

$$\underset{\overline{E}, \underline{E}, \overline{X}, \underline{X}, Z}{\text{Maximize}} \quad \pi = \overline{E} + \underline{E} + \overline{p}(\overline{X})\overline{X} + \underline{p}(\underline{X})\underline{X} - c(\overline{X} + \underline{X}) - rk(X + Z)$$

$$\text{subject to } \overline{E} \leq \int_0^{\overline{X}} \overline{p}(\overline{X}) d\overline{X} - \overline{p}(\overline{X})\overline{X} \qquad (13)$$

$$\underline{E} = \int_0^{\underline{X}} \underline{p}(\underline{X}) d\underline{X} - \underline{p}(\underline{X})\underline{X}$$

$$\pi \leq (s-r)k(\overline{X} + Z)$$

## 104  Regulation in Further Perspective

The constraints on the entrance fees assert that these cannot exceed the accumulated consumers surplus above the marginal usage charge to the particular customers. For, otherwise, the customer would purchase none of this particular product or service. If $\bar{\alpha}$ and $\underline{\alpha}$ denote the Lagrange multipliers for the entrance fee constraints, the Lagrangian for model (13) becomes

$$\phi(\bar{E},\underline{E},\bar{X},\underline{X},Z,\lambda,\bar{\alpha},\underline{\alpha}) = (1-\lambda)[\bar{E}+\underline{E}+\bar{p}(\bar{X})\bar{X}+\underline{p}(\underline{X})\underline{X}-c(\bar{X}+\underline{X})$$
$$- rk(\bar{X}+Z)] + \lambda(s-r)k(\bar{X}+Z)$$
$$+ \bar{\alpha}\left[\int_0^{\bar{X}} \bar{p}(\bar{X})d\bar{X} - \bar{p}(\bar{X})\bar{X} - \bar{E}\right]$$
$$+ \underline{\alpha}\left[\int_0^{\underline{X}} \underline{p}(\underline{X})d\underline{X} - \underline{p}(\underline{X})\underline{X} - \underline{E}\right]. \quad (14)$$

The Kuhn-Tucker conditions are

$$\phi_{\bar{E}}: \quad 1-\lambda \leq \bar{\alpha}, \bar{E}(1-\lambda-\bar{\alpha}) = 0 \quad (15)$$

$$\phi_{\underline{E}}: \quad 1-\lambda \leq \underline{\alpha}, \underline{E}(1-\lambda-\underline{\alpha}) = 0 \quad (16)$$

$$\phi_{\bar{X}}: \quad (1-\lambda)\left[\bar{p}(\bar{X})+\bar{X}\frac{d\bar{p}}{d\bar{X}}-c-rk\right] + \lambda(s-r)k - \bar{\alpha}\left[\bar{X}\frac{d\bar{p}}{d\bar{X}}\right] = 0 \quad (17)$$

$$\phi_{\underline{X}}: \quad (1-\lambda)\left[\underline{p}(\underline{X})+\underline{X}\frac{d\underline{p}}{d\underline{X}}-c\right] - \underline{\alpha}\left[\underline{X}\frac{d\underline{p}}{d\underline{X}}\right] = 0 \quad (18)$$

$$\phi_Z: \quad -rk + \lambda sk \leq 0, Zk(-r+\lambda s) = 0 \quad (19)$$

$$\phi_{\bar{\alpha}}: \quad \bar{E} \leq \int_0^{\bar{X}} \bar{p}(\bar{X})d\bar{X} - \bar{p}(\bar{X})\bar{X}, \bar{\alpha}\left[\bar{E} - \int_0^{\bar{X}} \bar{p}(\bar{X})d\bar{X} - \bar{p}(\bar{X})\bar{X}\right] = 0 \quad (20)$$

$$\phi_{\underline{\alpha}}: \quad \underline{E} \leq \int_0^{\underline{X}} \underline{p}(\underline{X})d\underline{X} - \underline{p}(\underline{X})\underline{X}, \underline{\alpha}\left[\underline{E} - \int_0^{\underline{X}} \underline{p}(\underline{X})d\underline{X} - \underline{p}(\underline{X})\underline{X}\right] = 0 \quad (21)$$

$$\phi_\lambda: \quad \pi \leq (s-r)k(\bar{X}+Z), \lambda[\pi - (s-r)k(\bar{X}+Z)] = 0 \quad (22)$$

A number of interesting results emerge from these conditions. First, in the absence of regulation, $\lambda = 0$ and, from (15) and (16), $\bar{\alpha} = \underline{\alpha} = 1$. Then, by (20) and (21), *the firm sets the customer for each class of customers so as to precisely equal the entire area above the usage price and below the demand curve.* Substituting $\bar{\alpha} = \underline{\alpha} = 1$ into (17) and (18), and simplifying, we find

$$\overline{p}_T = c + rk \tag{23}$$

$$\underline{p}_T = c \tag{24}$$

so that *under a two-part tariff welfare pricing is preserved: the usage prices to the peak and off-peak customers just exactly compensate at the margin for their respective additional costs.* Stated differently, the elasticity terms that appeared in Equations (5) and (6) have disappeared, and the welfare maximization results of Section II have re-emerged.

This result holds also if $K'$ replaces $rk$ as the marginal cost of capacity. Thus, in decreasing average cost industries, a two-part tariff enables the firm to be financially viable without having to depart (optimally or otherwsie) from marginal cost pricing. Welfare pricing ($\overline{W}$ and $\underline{W}$ in Figure 6-2) is the outcome, and yet the firm is not supported by taxation out of the public treasury.[15] *The two-part tariff is indeed "perfect" both in extracting all of the consumers' surplus, and because the investment decision, consumption decision, and resource allocation decision are all made at the correct margin.* However, the income distribution is now very different, since the utility has captured all of the social surplus[16] (the peak surplus $A\overline{Wp}_W$ in Figure 6-2 plus the off-peak surplus $E\underline{Wp}_W$ less the capacity deficit $B\overline{Wp}_W$.

**Regulation of Rate of Return but not of Price Structure.** One way to redistribute the income is to impose a rate-of-return constraint. Such a constraint has been included in Model (13). The model is thus one in which the regulator permits the firm to set its own price structure and insists only that the rate of return end up at the level deemed fair. When regulation is effective, $0 < \lambda < 1$ from (19). From (15) and (16), this means that $\overline{\alpha}$ and $\underline{\alpha}$ are both nonzero, so that the equalities must hold in the entrance fee constraints (20) and (21): as before, the customer charges are set so as to absorb the entire surplus.

If we solve for the off-peak usage price by substituting $\underline{\alpha} = 1 - \lambda$ into (18), we achieve the same result as (24): the off-peak user is charged his marginal running cost. To solve for the peak price, substitute $\overline{\alpha} = 1 - \lambda$ into (17) to obtain

$$\overline{p}_R = c + rk - \frac{1}{1-\lambda}(s-r)k \tag{25}$$

Hence, the price to the peak user is set below the sum of marginal operating and capacity costs and *capacity will always be in excess of the welfare-maximizing level.* In essence, the regulated utility absorbs the surplus from the customer charges entirely by expanding capacity.

This expansion of capacity will be productive as long as $\overline{p}_R > c$. To see this, note that if waste is positive ($Z > 0$), then $\lambda = r/s$, so that from (17), price must have been driven down to marginal operating cost. As long as price is

## 106 Regulation in Further Perspective

above this marginal cost, the firm prefers to add productive capacity, for by doing so it is simultaneously earning a larger surplus from the peak customer charge and is adding to the rate base. If price is below marginal running costs, then a deficit is incurred on marginal operation and it is cheaper, as long as the regulator permits $Z$ to enter the rate base, for the firm to add unused capital.

These results indicate that, *if the regulator does not distinguish productive from nonproductive capital, the pricing reversal discussed in previous sections cannot occur.* The price to off-peak users is set equal to marginal operating cost, and the price to the peak user is set above or equal to this level.

Figure 6-4 displays the equilibrium graphically. The regulated firm sets the same off-peak customer charge (equal to the area of the triangle $BJ\underline{p}_R$) and the same price, $\bar{p}_T$ as the unregulated firm. The off-peak surplus, along with that of the peak users (given by the triangle $A\overline{Wp}_W$) yield profits in excess of those allowed at the welfare-maximizing level of capacity, i.e., $A\overline{Wp}_W + BJ\underline{p}_R > HF\overline{Wp}_W$. Hence, the utility lowers peak price and expands capacity until at capacity $\bar{X}_R$ the total profit has been reduced (by the dotted triangle $\overline{WER}$) sufficiently to bring about equality in the regulatory constraint. The equilibrium price $\bar{p}_R$ is clearly below the welfare-maximizing level.

**Regulation of Price Structure.** In practice, the fixed charges levied by utilities appear to fall far short of the full consumer's surpluses. It is likely

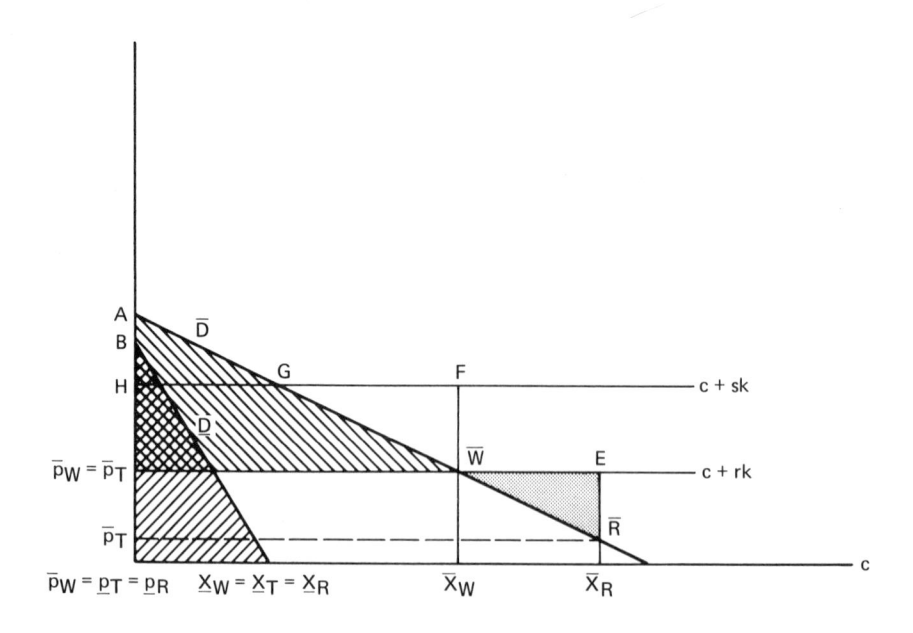

**Figure 6-4.** Two-Part Tariff and Rate-of-Return Regulation

*Reversals in Peak and Offpeak Prices* 107

that there are formal or informal limits imposed by regulators on the fixed charges that can be levied.[17] Let us suppose that the customer fees are set so as to take into account the large fixed capital costs in the industries, but that they are limited to levels below those at which all the surplus is absorbed. The interesting feature of the analysis when we construct the model in this way is that we revert to conclusions that closely resemble those in Section III. The elasticities of the different classes of customers are again evident, and the pricing reversal possibility reappears.

Figure 6-5 illustrates the situation. The customer charge to the offpeak user is assumed to be limited by the regulator to area $AGB$. A profit-maximizing firm does not set usage price equal to marginal operating cost for this off-peak period, but instead sets marginal revenue equal to cost, for by doing so, the off-peak surplus $\underline{p}_S MUQ$ can be gained in addition to the customer charge, $AGB$. It is for this reason that the elasticity effects show up in the first-order conditions.[18]

Similarly, the firm will treat the customer fee of the peak users, triangle $LOH$ in Figure 6-5, as an endowment of profit, and will proceed to adjust the usage price to the peak user until the regulatory constraint is satisfied. If the fair return is such that the profit permitted by the constraint is given by rectangle $NEGK$, then this rectangle must equal the sum of the surplus from the customer charges $AGB + LOH$, the surplus from the off-peak usage charge,

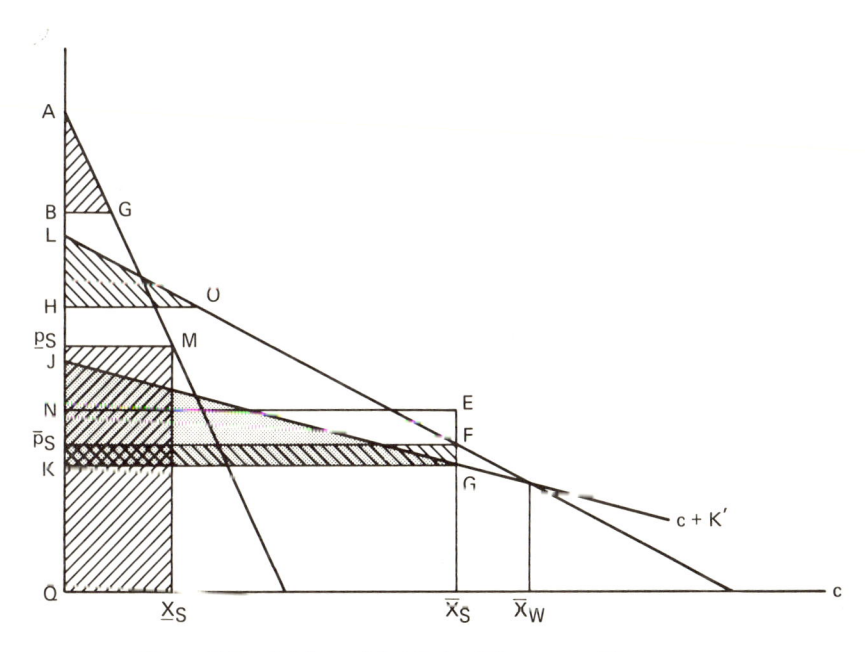

Figure 6-5. Pricing with Limited Customer Charge

$\underline{p_S}MUQ$, the deficit or surplus from the peak period (the surplus $\overline{p_S}FGK$), less the deficit $JGK$ incurred by the increasing returns to capacity, that is, $NEGK = AGB + LOH + \underline{p_S}MUQ + \overline{p_S}FGK - JGK$.

## V. Summary

We have demonstrated in this paper that it is theoretically possible for off-peak prices to be higher than peak prices for an unconstrained profit-maximizing firm, for a welfare-maximizing firm with increasing returns to scale, for a profit-maximizing firm subject to a regulatory constraint on its rate of return and for a firm that can levy a two-part tariff but where there is a constraint on the size of its customer charge. In the first two instances, the pricing reversal comes about because of the inverse elasticity rule, familiar from the optimal departures from marginal cost pricing literature. In the latter cases, the reversal comes about because the rate-of-return constraint encourages price reductions to peak-period users rather than to off-peak users. As a result, the pricing reversal becomes ever more likely to occur as the constraint is tightened. Furthermore, as the constraint is tightened, it becomes more likely that there can be an expansion of capacity beyond the welfare-maximizing level.

In the electricity example, these last results imply that for customer charges of approximately the same size, state regulatory agencies that have tighter rate-of-return requirements may encourage lower usage prices to peak business users while the prices charged to off-peak residential users remain substantially unchanged. An additional implication is that effectively regulated privately owned electric utilities might grant larger price reductions for business users than those instituted by government-owned electrics.

Either of these views suggest a possible method of empirically testing whether actual behavior in the electric utility industry agrees with that predicted by the theoretical models of peak-load pricing reversals. Recent evidence confirms that such agreement may be found. Peltzman, in contrasting the behavior of regulated and government-owned electrics finds that "residential output is about one third greater . . . (while) industrial output is twice as large in privately owned as in government-owned utilities . . . (so that) the magnitude of the output effect of ownership is, in fact, smallest for residential customers."[19] The relatively larger price reductions to the business users in the regulated electrics is just what our theory would predict.

**NOTES TO CHAPTER SIX**

    1. See, especially, Boiteux (1960), Steiner (1957, 1971), Hirshleifer (1958), Wellisz (1963), Williamson (1966), Turvey (1968), Littlechild (1970), Mohring (1970), and Pressman (1970). References are listed at the end of this paper.

    2. In essence, we have a model of price discrimination in which

demands are sequential rather than simultaneous. For a suggestive daily load curve showing that the electricity example fits this description in at least an approximative manner, see *Electric Power and Government Policy* (1948), p. 38. Of course, in practice peaks in the electric utilities are always attributable, at least in part, to both business and to residential customers.

3. Davidson (1955), p. 215. Notice also that the pricing reversal might be explained if the cost of distributing electricity to the residential customers (the $c$ term) were higher than the distribution cost to the business customer. See, for example MacAvoy and Noll (1973). Another complication that can arise in the real situation is that the peak and off-peak periods of the generating and distribution systems might occur at different times.

4. See Mohring (1970) for another discussion of this problem, which neglects, however, the pricing reversal phenomenom. See also Mowery (1970).

5. These rules are essentially the same as those derived in the more general model of optimal departures from marginal cost pricing, as described in Baumol and Bradford (1970) and Boiteux (1971). It is no accident that pricing rules of the Baumol and Bradford variety have appeared in our model. By implicitly assuming that we know which of the periods is peak and which is off-peak (as we have in our models), it has been possible to avoid explicit introduction of the capacity constraints, $\underline{X} \leq X$ and $X \leq \overline{X}$. This is precisely the trick that is needed to reduce the peak-load problem to a special case of an optimal departures from marginal cost pricing problem.

6. The idea that the firm might choose to operate off its production possibility frontier in a peak-load pricing model also appears in Riley (1972). See also Zajac (1972). In model (10) the regulator is assumed not to be able to distinguish between $\overline{X}$ and $Z$ and thus permits a fair return $s$ on either type of capital expense. If the regulator is instead assumed to detect and disallow all $Z$, the conclusions change slightly, as we will shortly show.

7. Note, however, that if there are cross-elasticities, the solution to (12) depends on the value of $s$, since there is a term coupling peak and off-peak demands

$$\overline{X} \frac{\partial \overline{p}}{\partial \underline{X}}.$$

Hence, the act of regulation may be expected to affect off-peak quantity and price in any case where a customer utilizes the service in both peak and off-peak periods.

8. See Wellisz (1963) for the earliest treatment of this matter.

9. In the more general case where each class of customers uses the facilities during both peak and off-peak periods, the regulatory constraint will almost certainly affect off-peak prices to at least some extent (see, for example, Bailey (1972) and Currie (1973) ).

10. Kafoglis (1971) also recognizes the possibility that expansions in capacity beyond the welfare maximizing level can occur in regulatory models when there is price discrimination between classes of customers.

11. A similar sort of result is derived in Bailey (1973, Chapters 6 and 8) in which it is shown that in an Averch-Johnson (1962) model of rate-of-return regulation the optimal capital stock increases as the fair return $s$ is lowered toward $r$, but does not change if the regulator holds $s$ fixed and the cost of capital $r$ fluctuates with changes in market conditions.

12. The Kuhn-Tucker conditions on $Z$ are that $k(-r + \lambda s) \leq 0$, and that $Zk(-r + \lambda s) = 0$.

13. Of course, if the regulator detects and disallows unproductive capital, such expenditures only subtract from profits and do not add to the rate base. In this case, adding productive capital would always be preferable.

14. This is the same sort of assumption as is made in MacAvoy and Noll (1973). The cases where customers have different demand curves and/or where entrance fees can be tailored to individual customers have been described in Oi (1971); however, Oi does not include peak and off-peak pricing considerations.

15. This point was made by Coase (1970), p. 118 and by Buchanan (1966), p. 470; also, see Oi (1971), and Buchanan (1953). Wallace Oates pointed out to us that for those in the field of public finance, welfare maximization implies a "regulatory" policy which actually leads to the welfare-maximizing outcome, which of course is precisely what happens in the two-part tariff situation.

16. For an interesting treatment of income distribution in this context, see Feldstein (1972).

17. These limits may arise in part because customers have different demand curves. In order to make the service available to everyone, the entrance fee cannot exceed the level which the customer with the smallest consumers' surplus is willing to pay. See Oi (1971).

18. More specifically, inspection of Equations (15) - (22) indicates that if $\bar{E}$ and $\underline{E}$ are limited to amounts unrelated to the elasticities of demands, these elasticities will reappear in the first order conditions determining the prices for peak and off-peak service. Elasticity effects would only be modified if the regulator permitted the customer fee to be in excess of a monopoly surplus triangle such as $AMp_R$ in Figure 6-5.

19. Peltzman (1971), p. 138. Strictly speaking, as Peltzman pointed out to us in correspondence, his "result was based upon more finely developed price discrimination by private as opposed to public utilities, rather than upon any difference in average residential and industrial rates." However, he goes on to state "the thrust of your argument seems to me to imply that regulated utilities will be motivated to seek special rates for the more elastic demands within as well as between customer groups."

## REFERENCES TO CHAPTER SIX

Harvey Averch and Leland L. Johnson, "Behavior of the Firm Under Regulatory Constraint," *American Economic Review*, December 1962, *52*, 1053-69.

Elizabeth E. Bailey, "Peak Load Pricing Under Regulatory Constraint," *Journal of Political Economy*, July/August 1972, *80*, 662-679.

Elizabeth E. Bailey, *Economic Theory of Regulatory Constraint*, Lexington Books, D.C. Heath and Company, 1973.

William J. Baumol and David F. Bradford, "Optimal Departures From Marginal Cost Pricing," *American Economic Review*, June 1970, *60*, 265-283.

Marcel Boiteux, "Peak-Load Pricing," *Journal of Business*, April 1960, *33*, 157-79.

Marcel Boiteux, "On the Management of Public Monopolies Subject to Budgetary Constraints," *Journal of Economic Theory*, September 1971, *3*, 219-40.

James M. Buchanan, "The Theory of Monopolistic Quantity Discounts," *Review of Economic Studies*, 1952-53, *20*, 199-208.

James M. Buchanan, "Peak Loads and Efficient Pricing: Comment," *Quarterly Journal and Economics*, August 1966, *80*, 472-80.

Ronald H. Coase, "The Theory of Public Utility Pricing and its Application," *Bell Journal of Economics and Management Science*, Spring 1970, *1*, 113-128.

Kent A. Currie, "Peak Load Pricing Under Regulatory Constraint: Comment," Manuscript, 1973.

Ralph K. Davidson, *Price Discrimination in Selling Gas and Electricity* (Baltimore: Johns Hopkins Press, 1955).

*Electric Power and Government Policy* (New York: The Twentieth Century Fund, 1948).

Martin S. Feldstein, "Equity and Efficiency in Public Sector Pricing: The Optimal Two-Part Tariff," *Quarterly Journal of Economics*, May 1972, *86*, 175-187.

Jack Hirshleifer, "Peak Loads and Efficient Pricing: Comment," *Quarterly Journal of Economics*, March 1951, *61*, 451-62.

Milton Z. Kafoglis, "Comment" in Harry M. Trebing (ed.) *Essays on Public Utility Pricing and Regulation* (East Lansing: Michigan State University, 1971).

Steven C. Littlechild, "Peak Load Pricing of Telephone Calls," *Bell Journal of Economics and Management Science*, Autumn 1970, *1*, 191-210.

Paul W. MacAvoy and Roger Noll, "Relative Prices on Regulated Transactions of the Natural Gas Pipelines," *Bell Journal of Economics and Management Science*, Spring 1973, *4*, 212-234.

Herbert Mohring, "The Peak Load Problem with Increasing Returns and Pricing Constraints," *American Economic Review*, September 1970, *60*, 693-705.

Vincent O. Mowery, "Optimal Pricing Theories for Interrelated Monopoly Outputs," Bell Laboratories Technical Memorandum, November 1970.

Walter Y. Oi, "A Disneyland Dilemma: Two-Part Tariffs for A Mickey Mouse Monopoly," *Quarterly Journal of Economics*, February 1971, *85*, 77-96.

Sam Peltzman, "Pricing in Public and Private Enterprises: Electric Utilities in the United States," *Journal of Law and Economics*, April 1971, 14, 109-147.

Israel Pressman, "Peak Load Pricing," *Bell Journal of Economics and Management Science*, Autumn 1970, *1*, 304-26.

John G. Riley, "Peak Load Pricing Under Regulatory Constraint: Comment," Manuscript, 1972.

Peter O. Steiner, "Peak Loads and Efficient Pricing," *Quarterly Journal of Economics*, November 1957, *71*, 585-610.

Peter O. Steiner, "Peak Load Pricing Revisited," in Harry M. Trebing (ed.) *Essays on Public Utility Pricing and Regulation*, (East Lansing: Michigan State University, 1971).

Ralph Turvey, "Peak-Load Pricing," *Journal of Political Economy*, January/February 1968, *76*, 107-113.

Stanislaw H. Wellisz, "Regulation of Natural Gas Pipeline Companies: An Economic Analysis," *Journal of Political Economy*, February 1963, *71*, 30-43.

Oliver E. Williamson, "Peak Load Pricing and Optimal Capacity Under Indivisibility Constraints," *American Economic Review*, September 1966, *56*, 810-27.

Edward E. Zajac, "Note on 'Gold Plating' or 'Rate Base Padding,' " *Bell Journal of Economics and Management Science*, Spring 1972, *3*, 311-5.

Chapter Seven

# A Method for Setting Norms in Regulated Industries

Barbara B. Murray

In the unregulated sector of the private economy, management has traditionally been concerned with the costs and revenues associated with the firm's product mix and with evaluating management performance. In this sector revenues are the "carrot" and costs are the "stick" for efficiently allocating resources to meet the market demands of consumers.

By contrast, in the regulated sector of the private economy, regulatory policy has focused primarily upon costs as the means of regulating utility company earnings. The emphasis is upon determining what are the legitimate outlay costs for labor, materials, interest charges on debt capital, and a "fair rate of return" on equity capital. Upon determination of these costs, a rate level necessary to cover these costs is approved. This is essentially a regulatory policy designed to establish rates upon the basis of a cost-plus pricing formula. It appears that if there is agreement on legitimate costs, with the implicit assumption that they are economically justified, then the company should maintain its service mix and cost allocations and earn revenue to cover the costs incurred. If the company has increasing average costs, this provides an incentive for a rate increase; whereas if costs are decreasing there is occasion to reduce rates. This regulatory policy of cost-plus pricing provides negative incentives by reversing the roles of revenues and costs, making costs the "carrot" and revenues the "stick." The burden is placed upon the commission to allow revenues to cover costs, rather than upon the company to adjust its service mix and costs to a given revenue objective or goal.

The precedent for this regulatory behavior pattern was established in the Smyth vs. Ames case of 1898. The important part of the opinion, which became the basis of the fair value doctrine, was the statement by which confiscation could be judged. This portion of the opinion reversed the issue of reasonable earnings into an issue of reasonable property valuations.

In the Hope Natural Gas case of 1944, the Court developed the end result criteria that shifted the focus to earnings. Justice Douglas wrote: "Under the statutory standard of 'just and reasonable' it is the end result reached not the method employed which is controlling. It is not theory but the impact of the rate order that counts. If the total effect of the rate order cannot be said to be unjust and unreasonable, judicial inquiry under the Act is at an end. The fact that the method employed to reach that result may contain some infirmities is not then important."[1] But there was still the problem of defining a norm for judging the reasonableness of the rate order with respect to both revenues and costs and providing incentives and sanctions for company performance.

### A Proposed Norm

If the consuming public is ultimately to pay for costs incurred by utilities, there should be some norm for identifying those components of the changes in costs for which they should or should not be held responsible. By the same token, regulatory commissions need to have a norm with respect to costs and revenues that will provide some way of measuring the desired performance of the company with respect to its service mix.

In developing a norm for evaluating cost performance, the total change has to be disaggregated into those components that are determined primarily by local factors, those that are a result of the average industry growth, and those that are a result of individual industry growth rates for particular services. We want to know the components that account for the actual change in costs incurred for individual services. This necessitates the determination of a base for measuring deviations. One common base for measuring deviation by individual firms is the industry. Therefore, the measures of cost performance become: (1) industry-wide average growth rate of costs for all services; (2) the degree to which costs for individual services are changing locally, compared to the same services industry-wide; and (3) which individual service costs are increasing at a faster or slower rate than the industry average.

The first measure is the expected costs associated with a service. If there are no differences in the particular characteristics of the local operating unit and regulatory commission, the individual services of a local unit should have a cost increase equal to the average industry growth rate for all service costs. In effect, the expected change in costs is the change that would occur if each service of the local unit should have gains or losses proportional to the industry rate.[2]

In actuality differences exist between local markets, local managements, and commissions. Consequently, actual changes in costs will deviate from expected changes. The deviations are a result of the "share" and "mix" factors associated with the costs of the service. The share factor measures the degree to which the costs associated with a service are increasing at a faster or slower rate locally compared to the rate for that *same* service at the industry level.[3] The mix factor identifies those services for which costs are increasing at a faster or slower rate than the industry's rate for all services.[4] When an operating unit shows a negative mix factor for costs, it is still contributing to total costs; but it has a damping effect upon the rate of increase in total costs.

### Regulatory Policies and "Mix and Share"

Expected growth is determined by industrial and national factors; consequently local managements and commissions have little or no control over this component of costs. The mix factor, which is also determined by industry forces, can be used as a variable for local control by local managements and commissions. This would be via adjustments of the overall service mix rather than the mix factor for individual services—the introduction of new services and/or abandonment of existing services. The share factor, however, is the key variable for measuring the performance of local management and for providing a policy tool to commissions; for it is the share factor which indicates whether costs, associated with individual services, are increasing at rates above or below the industry rate for a given service.

The identification of the mix and share components of costs are essential for regulatory policies designed to provide continuous surveillance, incentives, and performance evaluation to be workable. Analysis of mix and share components, however, requires more of a micro approach to rate making than has traditionally been exercised by commissions.

Commissions and managements will have to look more closely at the components of the changes in the costs of individual services. Correspondingly, under cost-plus pricing, commissions would have more control over the prices of individual services and could provide stronger incentives for local management performance. The policy implications of mix and share analysis with respect to continuous surveillance, pricing, incentives for local management, and identification of problem areas will now be discussed.

### Continuous Surveillance

The current procedures in rate making require extended time periods before a "solution" is determined with respect to rate levels. William Shepherd feels that this regulatory lag "has been extensive enough to offer substantial incentives for cost reductions and discouragement to cost inflation."[5] Others, such as Thomas Gies, feel that the current procedural methods should be modified in favor of *continuous surveillance* "which . . . will accomodate more successfully to the consideration of innovation in measurement of utility performance."[6] If continuous surveillance is to be effective, it must provide a workable and speedy method for analyzing the data that are collected.

The norms previously presented provide a feasible means for quickly evaluating the large amounts of data gathered over time for objectively evaluating company performance *over time*. Certainly both commissions and management need to know if costs are increasing because of industry factors (the mix effects) or because of local factors (the share effect) in order to develop various policy alternatives.

If cost data were submitted in terms of this analysis, as well as the traditional actual changes, commissions and management could continuously review the company's performance and revenue requirements. Rather than formal full-dress hearings, informal hearings, could be used to evaluate rate changes and cost control measures. This would reduce the regulatory lag and "lumpiness" of rate changes that exist under the current procedures and methods of data presentation. By identifying mix and share components of costs there could be incremental changes in rates reflecting industry factors and local management performance with respect to individual services.

As Gies notes, "The more fully informed the commission is able to make itself, the less purely 'educational' work is necessary at the time of the decision, and therefore the more likely it is that the commissioners can direct fullest attention to *interpretation* and *appraisal* rather than merely assembling and assimilating the facts." In order to interpret, the commission has to first disaggregate the cost data with respect to its expected growth, mix and share factors in order to "explain" the changes not only of total costs but also the total costs associated with individual services. In order to appraise the disaggregated data, the commission should know which components, such as the share factor, measure management performance in its local market. If data were presented in terms of this analysis, the degree of conflict could be reduced with respect to what are allowable costs for cost-plus pricing, and incentives and sanctions with respect to pricing could be provided. The following section illustrates the use of the mix and share components for regulatory policy and for providing management incentives under cost-plus pricing.

### Incentives and Evaluation with Respect to Mix and Share

When cost data are presented in terms of the expected growth, mix and share components, commissions are in a position to provide incentives for management performance. Since the expected growth and mix factors of the change in costs for a service are beyond local management and commission control, this portion of costs would have to be allowed under cost-plus pricing. The primary decisions with respect to services with positive mix factors are: (1) whether the above average increase in costs of the service can be offset with a negative share factor of costs; (2) whether services with negative mix factors can be provided thereby offsetting the positive mix factor so that the change in total costs is the same as the industry; and (3) whether the service should be continued or abandoned.

If the mix factor and expected growth factor are allowable costs, then the share factor becomes the primary policy tool for commissions to provide incentives and evaluate management performance. Let us assume two cases illustrating the share component as a policy tool, one a service with a negative share factor, the other one with a positive share factor.

In the first case, local management's performance is better than that of the industry; its increases in costs for the same service are below those of the industry. If management is to be "rewarded" for its better performance, it should be allowed a larger net revenue for this service than that for the industry, a larger mark-up over costs under cost-plus pricing. If commissions require a reduction in rates for the service, because of below average increases in costs locally, there is no incentive for management to control local costs, but rather to increase cost.

In the second case, where there is a positive share factor for the costs associated with the service, costs for the service are increasing more rapidly locally than for the industry. The question here is: Should the commission allow the full share component of the costs to be covered by a rate increase? The commission and local management would have to address themselves to the reasons for the positive share factor. Some of the possible causes could be: (1) poor management; (2) local labor market characteristics; and (3) population and demand distributions. That portion which is attributed to poor management performance would not be allowed in the determination of the revenue requirement. This would provide an incentive for management to improve its performance rather than have the consuming public pay for poor management with respect to local costs.

### Identification of Problem Areas

It is difficult for commissions to hold rates down under cost-plus pricing when the services of the operating unit consist primarily of services showing positive mix factors for costs. The positive mix factor acts as a drag upon the reduction of the change in overall costs. Although local management may be able to offset a portion of the mix component, it is unlikely that they would be able to completely negate the positive mix component for each service with a negative share factor. Consequently, it is necessary for commissions and management to identify possible problem areas for which policy decisions have to be made.

Some of the problem areas for which this analysis could be utilized are: (1) abandonment of services; (2) the overall mix of services; and (3) poor revenue performance associated with specific services. When a utility service is initiated it tends to become institutionalized. Commissions are reluctant to withdraw or abandon the service. This analysis provides a means for identifying services that could be candidates for abandonment, or if they are to be maintained, the corresponding drag and cross subsidization associated with their continuation.

A service would be a candidate for abandonment, if the change in the demand for the service should have negative mix and share factors in conjunction with positive mix and share factors for its costs. In other words, not only is the service a slow-growing, high-cost service for the industry, but local increase in demand is less than that for the industry, and local costs are increasing at a faster rate than that of the indusr consideration would be the revenues associated with the service. If revenues also have negative mix and share components and are less than the mix and share components of costs, there is cross-subsidization of the service. On the basis of efficiency, the case can be made for abandonment. But if, as is often the case, equity considerations are used to maintain the service, the costs and degree of cross-subsidization associated with implementation of the service can be identified, and compared to the benefits in order to reach a policy decision.

In some instances, total costs for local units increase at a higher rate than those of the industry. As previously noted, this may be the result of poor management and be identified by positive share factors. Conversely, a higher rate of increasing costs may also be caused because the unit offers a majority of services with costs increasing at a faster rate than the general industry rate for all services. These "high cost services" can be identified by their positive mix factors for cost coupled with near zero share factors. Under these circumstances it should be the responsibility of the commission and management to review the service mix, leading hopefully to balancing the overall mix factor by introducing services with negative mix factors. This could be accomplished by the introduction of additional industry services, new to the local market, that have negative mix factors for costs. Another alternative would be to allow regulated firms to compete with non-regulated firms in offering services with negative mix factors for costs.

With respect to the third problem area, previously identified as poor revenue performance, it is also possible to analyze mix and share factors associated with individual services. If individual services show negative mix and share factors for revenues, under demand pricing, then the introduction of new services would not only require negative mix factors but also positive revenue mix and share factors. This would mean that there would be cross subsidization of services within the total service mix.

Another aspect of the revenue problem arises when the share factor associated with individual services is negative. This implies that either local commission control over rates or local demand-distributions and characteristics are insufficient for the local operating unit to perform at the industry rate for the service. If the revenue share factors associated with services are negative, commissions and management should review pricing policies and/or allowable rates for the service so that a revenue growth equal to the industry rate for the service could be achieved. Such a result would be indicated when the revenue share factor for the service reached zero.

## Summary

If commissions are to effectively evaluate local management performance and provide positive incentives, objective norms need to be developed. This paper presents a methodology for developing such norms, the mix and share factors associated with the changes in costs of individual services. The same methodology can be applied to revenues and service outputs for identifying which portion of the total change is due to industry factors and which portion to local factors.

Because of the simplicity of the methodology it can be readily used under a continuous surveillance procedure for measuring and evaluating utility performance. It would reduce the regulatory lag and the lumpiness of rate changes existing under current procedures.

The share factor is the primary variable for providing incentives and evaluating company performance. It is this factor that provides the "carrot" under cost-plus pricing. The identification of the mix factor could reduce the degree of conflict in rate hearings. Inasmuch as this factor is determined by industry forces, it would be an allowable portion of costs.

The proposed methodology is also applicable to the identification of problem areas. Examples of these are the abandonment of services, adjustment of the service mix, and poor revenue performance.

The primary policy implication of the methodology is that it identifies that component of the total change in costs, or other variables such as revenues and output, that are primarily determined locally. This implies that a micro approach to rate making, with respect to individual services, can be used by commissions and management. Some possible policy applications are: (1) quantitative identification of services for abandonment for equity decisions; (2) allowing larger net revenues by various pricing policies for services where management has a negative share factors for costs; (3) allowing local firms to introduce new industry services that would offset a predominance of services with positive mix factors for costs; and (4) adjusting the balance of the mix factors associated with the costs of the service mix by allowing regulated firms to compete with non-regulated firms for services with negative mix factors for costs and positive mix factors for revenues.

It should be emphasized that this analysis only factors out the components of a given change. It does not explicitly provide the behavioral or policy alternatives. It only provides the starting point for interpretation and analysis for rational policy making.

### An Application to Michigan Bell and New England Bell.

This method of analysis was used to indicate the per telephone revenue performance of Michigan Bell and New England Bell relative to the Bell system for the various time intervals indicated in Table 7-1. The corresponding numerical components

Table 7-1. Operating Revenue Per Telephone Michigan Bell and New England Bell

| | 1940 1950 | | | 1941 1945 | | 1950 1960 | | 1951 1955 | | 1960 1965 | | 1960 1968 | | 1960 1970 | | 1961 1971 | | 1965 1971 | | |
|---|---|---|---|---|---|---|---|---|---|---|---|---|---|---|---|---|---|---|---|---|
| | Mix | Shr | Mix | Shr | Mix | Shr | Mix | Shr | Mix | Shr | Mix | Shr | Mix | Shr | Mix | Shr | Mix | Shr | |
| Local Service | − | − | − | − | − | − | − | − | − | + | − | + | − | − | − | − | − | − | Michigan Bell |
| | − | + | − | + | − | + | − | + | − | − | − | − | − | − | − | − | − | − | New England |
| Local Toll | + | + | + | + | + | − | + | + | + | − | + | + | + | + | + | + | + | + | Michigan |
| | + | + | − | − | + | + | + | + | + | − | + | + | + | + | + | + | + | + | New England |
| Miscellaneous | + | + | + | − | + | + | + | + | + | − | − | + | + | + | + | + | − | + | Michigan |
| | + | + | − | − | + | + | + | + | + | − | − | − | − | − | − | − | − | − | New England |
| Uncollectable Operating Revenue | − | 0 | − | − | + | + | 0 | + | − | − | + | − | + | − | + | − | + | + | Michigan |
| | − | − | − | + | + | + | 0 | + | − | + | + | + | + | + | + | + | + | + | New England |
| Total Operating Revenue | + | − | + | − | − | − | 0 | − | + | − | − | − | − | − | − | − | − | − | Michigan |
| | + | + | + | − | − | + | 0 | + | + | − | − | − | − | − | − | − | − | + | New England |
| Total (Gross Revenue) | − | − | − | − | − | − | − | − | − | − | − | − | − | − | − | − | − | − | Michigan |
| | − | − | − | − | + | + | + | + | − | − | − | − | − | − | − | − | + | + | New England |

for the mix, share, and growth factors during the 1965-1971 time interval are presented in Table 7-2.

These results indicate that local service revenues per telephone had a below average revenue growth for all the time intervals examined. The effect of this negative mix factor is to act as a "drag" upon the growth in total revenues. In addition, the negative share factor for these two operating units indicates a slower revenue growth for local service than that for Bell system. The effect of these factors is that although local service revenues per telephone for Michigan Bell had an increase of $9.25, it was accounted for primarily by the growth factor.

If local service per telephone had grown at the average rate for all revenues of the Bell system, there would have been a $19.90 increase. Because this was a slow growing source of revenues, there was a "paper loss" of $7.91 per telephone. In addition, the revenue performance of Michigan Bell was below that of the Bell system for local service resulting in a "loss" of $2.74 per telephone because of company and/or commission policies. Therefore, the net gain in revenues of $9.25 was due to the growth factor over which local commissions and management have no control.

The negative mix factor for local service revenues per telephone could be a reflection of a pricing policy designed to establish a low minimum rate for basic service so as to increase the number of stations and to generate revenues from other sources, such as toll service. This possibility may account for the positive mix factor for toll service revenues per telephone in all the time intervals. In addition to the above average growth of toll service revenues, these two operating units had above average revenue performance in their market

Table 7-2. Operating Revenues Per Telephone 1965-1971

| Michigan | 1965 | 1971 | Diff | Growth | Mix | Share |
|---|---|---|---|---|---|---|
| Local Serv Per Telep | 75.99 | 85.24 | 9.25 | 19.90 | −7.91 | −2.74 |
| Local Toll Per Telep | 34.86 | 53.89 | 19.03 | 9.13 | 5.12 | 4.78 |
| Misc Oper Per Telep | 8.08 | 9.78 | 1.70 | 2.12 | −0.85 | 0.44 |
| Total Rev Per Telep | 118.93 | 148.91 | 29.98 | 31.14 | 0.0 | −1.16 |
| Uncoll Rev Per Telep | 0.38 | 1.00 | 0.62 | 0.10 | 0.39 | 0.14 |
| Total Oper Per Telep | 118.55 | 147.91 | 29.36 | 31.04 | −0.55 | −1.13 |

Operating Revenues Per Telephone 1965-1971

| New England | 1965 | 1971 | Diff | Growth | Mix | Share |
|---|---|---|---|---|---|---|
| Local Serv Per Telep | 79.62 | 91.69 | 12.07 | 20.85 | −8.29 | −0.49 |
| Local Toll Per Telep | 48.85 | 76.56 | 27.71 | 12.79 | 7.17 | 7.75 |
| Misc Oper Per Telep | 5.87 | 6.66 | 0.79 | 1.54 | −0.62 | −0.13 |
| Total Rev Per Telep | 134.34 | 174.91 | 40.57 | 35.18 | 0.00 | 5.39 |
| Uncoll Rev Per Telep | 0.49 | 1.47 | 0.98 | 0.13 | 0.50 | 0.36 |
| Total Oper Per Telep | 133.85 | 173.44 | 39.59 | 35.05 | 0.62 | 5.17 |

areas. The actual increase for Michigan Bell of $19.03 in revenues per telephone was accounted for by a growth factor of $9.13, $5.12 because of the above average revenue growth of the service relative to all services, and $4.78 because of above average revenue growth for toll service locally as compared to toll service revenue growth for the Bell system.

Under the statewide bases of rate making, the approved revenue requirement is apportioned between local service and intrastate toll service. Consequently, intrastate toll service revenues are directly related to local service revenues. Considering the differences in the mix factors for these two services, it appears that the various state commissions in the Bell system require a larger portion of the statewide revenue requirement from toll service than from local service. The positive share factor for these two operating units would seem to indicate that their state commissions require an even greater proportion of the revenue requirement to be derived from toll service than the average for the Bell system.

**Uncollectible Revenues.** Beginning in 1960, uncollectible revenues per telephone grew faster than total revenues per telephone for the Bell system. Until the 1965-1971 time period, Michigan Bell was able to keep its growth rate in uncollectible revenues below that rate for the Bell system.

If Michigan Bell had the same performance as the Bell system for total revenue growth per telephone, the growth factor, uncollectible revenues would have increased by $.10 per telephone during the 1965-1971 period. But, because uncollectible revenues per telephone were increasing at a faster rate than total revenues, there was an additional increase of $.39 due to the mix factor. Compounding the unfavorable situation was the fact that uncollectible revenues were increasing at a faster rate in Michigan Bell's market, adding an additional $.14 per telephone. The sum of these components account for the actual $.62 revenue loss due to uncollectible revenues.

**Total Net Operating Revenues Per Telephone.** If both operating units had a revenue growth equal to the average for total gross revenues for the Bell system, revenues would have increased to $31.04 for Michigan Bell and $35.05 for New England Bell. But, actual total net revenues increased by $39.59 for New England Bell and $29.36 for Michigan Bell. The better revenue performance of New England Bell was due to its above average revenue performance in its market for total net revenue growth. This is accounted for by the $5.17 positive revenue share factor which more than offset the $.62 revenue drag due to the mix factor. In contrast, Michigan Bell's actual revenue per telephone were less than the expected growth. This was a result of loss of revenues of $1.13 because of poor performance in its market and also because of the $.52 revenue drag, due to the below average growth of total net operating revenues per telephone. As Emory Troxel noted in his study of telephone regulation in Michigan,

"... that the Michigan Commission puts strong constraints on telephone prices and revenues. Whatever else may be said about the Commission, it certainly makes large cuts in Bell Company requests for additional revenues."[8] The negative share factor for either total net or gross operating revenues per telephone supports his observations.

Both operating units showed below average revenues performance for total net and gross revenues per telephone for all the time intervals except for the 1965-1971 for New England Bell. This is essentially a growth problem as indicated by the mix and share factors. As William Shepherd noted in 1966, "... there are serious growth problems for telephone companies, both Bell and independent. Some important telephone markets are nearly "saturated," in that growth in basic services is insensitive to price and will continue only at about the rate of new household formation for the economy ... All of this points to relatively slow future growth in traditional telephone services, and it probably explains some strong efforts by larger telephone systems in particular to introduce optional services and diversify into areas with prospects for more rapid growth and technical advance."[9] This analysis of the growth, mix, and share factors for the various sources of revenue growth support his observation.

## NOTES TO CHAPTER SEVEN

1. Federal Power Commission v. Hope Natural Gas Company, 320 United States 591 (1944), p. 602.

2. The expected growth is:

$$G = \frac{C_T - C_{T-1}}{C_{t-1}} \times ci_{t-1}$$

where

$CT$ = industry costs for all service in period $t$
$CT-1$ = industry costs for all services in period $t-1$
$ci_{t-1}$ = local costs for service ($i$) in period $t-1$

3. The share factor is:

$$S = (ci_t - ci_{t-1}) \div \frac{Ci_T - Ci_{t-1}}{C_{t-1}} \times ci_{t-1}$$

where

$ci_t$ = local costs of service ($i$) in period $t$
$ci_t-1$ = local costs of service ($e$) in period $t-1$

4. The mix factor is:

$$M = (ci_t - ci_{t-1}) - (G+S)$$

where

$ci_t$ = local costs for service ($i$) in period ($t$)
$ci_{t-1}$ = local costs for service ($i$) in period $t-1$
$G$ = expected growth
$S$ = share

5. William G. Shepherd, "Utility Growth and Profits under Regulation," in *Utility Regulation: New Directions in Theory and Policies*, William G. Shepherd and Thomas G. Gies (editors), Random House, 1966, p. 31.

6. *Op. cit.*, Thomas G. Gies, "New Concepts in Public Utility Regulation," pp. 107-108.

7. *Ibid.*, p. 109.

8. Emory Troxel, "Telephone Regulation in Michigan," in *Utility Regulation: New Directions in Theory and Practice*, William G. Shepherd and Thomas G. Gies, Editors, Random House, 1966, p. 154.

9. *Op. cit.*, pp. 10-11.

Chapter Eight

# Why Regulate Utilities?

Harold Demsetz

Current economic doctrine offers to its students a basic relationship between the number of firms that produce for a given market and the degree to which competitive results will prevail.* Stated explicitly or suggested implicitly is the doctrine that price and output can be expected to diverge to a greater extent from their competitive levels the fewer the firms that produce the product for the market. This relationship has provided the logic that motivates much of the research devoted to studying industrial concentration, and it has given considerable support to utility regulation.[1]

In this chapter, I shall argue that the asserted relationship between market concentration and competition cannot be derived from existing theoretical considerations and that it is based largely on an incorrect understanding of the concept of competition or rivalry. The strongest application of the asserted relationship is in the area of utility regulation since, if we assume scale economies in production, it can be deduced that only one firm will produce the commodity. The logical validity or falsity of the asserted relationship should reveal itself most clearly in this case.

Although public utility regulation recently has been criticized because of its ineffectiveness or because of the undesirable indirect effects it produces, the basic intellectual arguments for believing that truly effective regulation is desirable have not been challenged.[2] Even those who are inclined to reject government regulation or ownership of public utilities because they believe these alternatives are more undesirable than private monopoly, implicitly accept the intellectual arguments that underlie regulation.[3]

---

*The author is indebted to R.H. Coase, who was unconvinced by the natural monopoly argument long before this paper was written, and to George J. Stigler and Joel Segall for helpful comments and criticisms. Reprinted with permission from the *Journal of Law & Economics*, April 1968.

125

The economic theory of natural monopoly is exceedingly brief and, we shall see, exceedingly unclear. Current doctrine is reflected in two recent statements of the theory. Samuelson writes:

> Under persisting decreasing costs for the firm, one or a few of them will so expand their q's as to become a significant part of the market for the industry's total Q. We would then end up (1) with a single monopolist who dominates the industry; (2) with a few large sellers who together dominate the industry ... or (3) with some kind of imperfection of competition that, in either a stable way or in connection with a series of intermittent price wars, represents an important departure from the economist's model of "perfect" competition wherein no firm has any control over industry price.[4]

Alchian and Allen view the problem as follows:

> If a product is produced under cost conditions such that larger rates ... (would) mean lower average cost per unit, ... only one firm could survive; if there were two firms, one could expand to reduce costs and selling price and thereby eliminate the other. In view of the impossibility of more than one firm's being profitable, two is too many. But if there is only one, that incumbent firm may be able to set prices above free-entry costs for a long time. Either resources are wasted because too many are in the industry, or there is just one firm, which will be able to charge monopoly prices.[5]

At this point it will be useful to state explicitly the interpretation of natural monopoly used in this paper. If, because of production scale economies, it is less costly for one firm to produce a commodity in a given market than it is for two or more firms, then one firm will survive; if left unregulated, that firm will set price and output at monopoly levels; the price-output decision of that firm will be determined by profit maximizing behavior constrained only by the market demand for the commodity.

The theory of natural monopoly is deficient for it fails to reveal the logical steps that carry it from scale economies in production to monopoly price in the market place. To see this most clearly, let us consider the contracting process from its beginning.

Why must rivals share the market? Rival sellers can offer to enter into contracts with buyers. In this bidding competition, the rival who offers buyers the most favorable terms will obtain their patronage; there is no clear or necessary reason for bidding rivals to share in the production of the goods and, therefore, there is no clear reason for competition in bidding to result in an increase in per-unit production costs.

Why must the unregulated market outcome be monopoly price? The competitiveness of the bidding process depends very much on such things as the number of bidders, but there is no clear or necessary reason for production scale economies to decrease the number of bidders. Let prospective buyers call for bids to service their demands. Scale economies in servicing their demands in no way imply that there will be one bidder only. There can be many bidders and the bid that wins will be the lowest. The existence of scale economies in the production of the service is irrelevant to a determination of the number of rival bidders. If the number of bidders is large or if, for other reasons, collusion among them is impractical, the contracted price can be very close to per-unit production cost.[6]

The determinants of competition in market negotiations differ from and should not be confused with the determinants of the number of firms from which production will issue after contractual negotiations have been completed. The theory of natural monopoly is clearly unclear. Economies of scale in production imply that the bids submitted will offer increasing quantities at lower per-unit costs, but production scale economies imply nothing obvious about how competitive these prices will be. If one bidder can do the job at less cost than two or more, because each would then have a smaller output rate, then the bidder with the lowest bid price for the entire job will be awarded the contract, whether the good be cement, electricity, stamp vending machines, or whatever; but the lowest bid price need not be a monopoly price.[7]

The criticism made here of the theory of natural monopoly can be understood best by constructing an example that is free from irrelevant complications, such as durability of distributions systems, uncertainty, and irrational behavior, all of which may or may not justify the use of regulatory commissions but none of which is relevant to the theory of natural monopoly; for this theory depends on one belief only—price and output will be at monopoly levels if, due to scale economies, only one firm succeeds in producing the product.

Assume that owners of automobiles are required to own and display new license plates each year. The production of license plates is subject to scale economies.

The theory of natural monopoly asserts that under these conditions the owners of automobiles will purchase plates from one firm only and that firm, in the absence of regulation, will charge a monopoly price, a price that is constrained only by the demand for and the cost of producing license plates. The logic of the example does dictate that license plates will be purchased from one firm because this will allow that firm to offer the plates at a price based on the lowest possible per-unit cost. But why should that price be a monopoly price?

There can be many bidders for the annual contract. Each will submit a bid based on the assumption that if its bid is lowest it will sell to all residents, if it is not lowest it sells to none. Under these conditions there will exist enough independently acting bidders to assure that the winning price will differ insignificantly from the per-unit cost of producing license plates.

If only one firm submits the lowest price, the process ends, but if two or more firms submit the lowest price, either one is selected according to some random selection device or else one is allowed to sell or give his contracts to the other. There is no monopoly price although there may be rent to some factors if their supply is positively sloped. There is no regulation of firms in the industry. The price is determined in the bidding market. The only role played by the government or by a consumers' buying cooperative is some random device to select the winning bidder if more than one bidder bids the lowest price.

There are only two important assumptions: (1) The inputs required to enter production must be available to many potential bidders at prices determined in open markets. This lends credibility to numerous rival bids. (2) The cost of colluding by bidding rivals must be prohibitively high. The reader will recognize that these requirements are no different than those required to avoid monopoly price in any market, whether production in that market is or is not subject to scale economies.

Moreover, if we are willing to consider the possibility that collusion or merger of all potential bidding rivals is a reasonable prospect, then we must examine the other side of the coin. Why should collusion or merger of buyers be prohibitively costly if an infinite or large number of bidding rivals can collude successfully? If we allow buyers access to the same technology of collusion, the market will be characterized by bilateral negotiations between organized buyers and organized sellers. While the outcome of such negotiations is somewhat uncertain with respect to wealth distribution, there is no reason to expect inefficiency.

Just what is the supply elasticity of bidders and what are the costs of colluding are questions to be answered empirically, since they cannot be deduced from production scale economies. There exist more than one firm in every public utility industry, and many firms exist in some public utility industries. This is true even though licensing restrictions have been severe; the assertion that the supply of potential bidders in any market would be very inelastic if licensing restrictions could be abolished would seem difficult to defend when producing competitors exist in nearby markets. The presence of active rivalry is clearly indicated in public utility history. In fact, producing competitors, not to mention unsuccessful bidders, were so plentiful that one begins to doubt that scale economies characterized the utility industry at the time when regulation replaced market competition. Complaints were common that the streets were too frequently in a state of disrepair for the purpose of accommodating competing companies. Behling writes:

> There is scarcely a city in the country that has not experienced competition in one or more of the utility industries. Six electric light companies were organized in the one year of 1887 in New York City. Forty-five electric light enterprises had the legal right to oper-

ate in Chicago in 1907. Prior to 1895, Duluth, Minnesota was served by five electric lighting companies, and Scranton, Pennsylvania, had four in 1906 . . . During the latter part of the nineteenth century, competition was the usual situation in the gas industry in this country. Before 1884, six competing companies were operating in New York City . . . Competition was common and especially persistent in the telephone industry. According to a special report of the Census in 1902, out of 1051 incorporated cities in the United States with a population of more than 4,000 persons, 1002 were provided with telephone facilities. The independent companies had a monopoly in 137 of the cities, the Bell interests had exclusive control over communication by telephone in 414 cities, while the remaining 451, almost half, were receiving duplicated service. Baltimore, Chicago, Cleveland, Columbus, Detroit, Kansas City, Minneapolis, Philadelphia, Pittsburgh, and St. Louis, among the larger cities, had at least two telephone services in 1905.[8]

It would seem that the number of potential bidding rivals in the public utility industries and the cost of their colluding are likely to be at least as great as in several other industries for which we find that unregulated markets work tolerably well.

The natural monopoly theory provides no logical basis for monopoly prices. The theory is illogical. Moreover, for the general case of public utility industries, there seems no clear evidence that the cost of colluding is significantly lower than it is for industries for which unregulated market competition seems to work. To the extent that utility regulation is based on the fear of monopoly price, merely because one firm will serve each market, it is not based on any deducible economic theorem.

The important point that needs stressing is that we have no theory that allows us to deduce from the observable degree of concentration in a particular market whether or not price and output are competitive. We have as yet no general theory of collusion and certainly not one that allows us to associate observed concentration in a particular market with successful collusion.[9]

It is possible to make some statements about collusion that reveal the nature of the forces at work. These statements are largely intuitive and cannot be pursued in detail here, but they may be useful in imparting to the reader a notion of what is meant by a theory of collusion. Let us suppose that there are no special costs to competing; that is, we assume that sellers do not need to keep track of the prices or other activities of their competitors. Second, assume that there are some costs of colluding that must be borne by members of a bidders' cartel. This condition is approximated least well where the government subsidizes the cost of colluding—for example, the United States Department of Agriculture. Finally, assume that there are no legal barriers to entry.

Under these conditions, new bidding rivals will be paid to join the collusion. In return for joining they will receive a pro rata share of monopoly profits. As more rivals appear the pro rata share must fall. The cartel will continue paying new rivals to join until the pro rata share falls to the cost of colluding. That is, until the cartel members receive a competitive rate of return for remaining in the cartel. The next rival bidder can refuse to join the cartel; instead he can enter the market at a price below the cartel price (as can any present member of the cartel who chooses to break away). If there is some friction in the system, this rival will choose this course of action in preference to joining the cartel, for if he joins the cartel he receives a competitive rate of return; whereas if he competes outside the cartel by selling at a price below that of the cartel, he receives an above-competitive rate of return for some short-run period. Under the assumed conditions the cartel must eventually fail and price and output can be competitive even though only a few firms actually produce the product. Moreover, the essential ingredient to its eventual failure is only that the private per-firm cost of colluding exceeds the private per-firm cost of competing.

Under what conditions will the cost of colluding exceed the cost of competing? How will these costs be affected by allowing coercive tactics? What about buyer cartels? What factors affect how long is "eventually"? Such questions remain to be answered by a theory of collusion. Until such questions are answered, public policy prescriptions must be suspect. A market in which many firms produce may be competitive or it may be collusive; the large number of firms merely reflects production scale diseconomies; large numbers do not necessarily reflect high or low collusion costs. A market in which few firms produce may be competitive or it may be collusive; the small number of firms merely reflects production scale economies; fewness does not necessarily reflect high or low collusion costs. Thus, an economist may view the many retailers who sell on "fair trade" terms with suspicion; and he may marvel at the ability of large numbers of workers to form effective unions; and yet, he may look with admiration at the performance of the few firms who sell airplanes, cameras, or automobiles.

The subject of monopoly price is necessarily permeated with the subject of negotiating or contracting costs. A world in which negotiating costs are zero is a world in which no monopolistic inefficiencies will be present, simply because buyers and sellers both can profit from negotiations that result in a reduction and elimination of inefficiencies. In such a world it will be bargaining skills and not market structures that determine the distribution of wealth. If a monopolistic structure exists on one side of the market, the other side of the market will be organized to offset any power implied by the monopolistic structure. The organization of the other side of the market can be undertaken by members of that side or by rivals of the monopolistic structure that prevails on the first side. The co-existence of monopoly power and monopoly structure is possible only if the costs of negotiating are differentially positive, being lower for one set of sellers (or buyers) than it is for rival sellers (or buyers). If one set of sellers (or buyers) can organize those on the other side of the market more cheaply than can rivals, then price may be raised (or lowered) to the extent of the existing differential advantage in negotiating costs; this extent generally will be less than the simple monopoly price. In some cases the differential advantage in negotiating costs may be so great that price will settle at the monopoly (monopsony) level. This surely cannot be the general case, but the likelihood of it surely increases as the costs imposed on potential rivals increase; legally restricting entry is one way of raising the differential disadvantages to rivals; the economic meaning of restricting entry is increasing the cost to potential rivals of negotiating with and organizing buyers (or sellers).

The public policy question is which groups of market participants, if any, are to receive governmentally sponsored advantages or disadvantages, not only in the subsidization or taxation of production but also in the creation of advantages or disadvantages in conducting negotiations.

At this juncture, it should be emphasized that I have argued not that regulatory commissions are undesirable but that economic theory does not, at present, provide a justification for commissions insofar as they are based on the belief that observed concentration and monopoly price bear any necessary relationship.

Indeed, in utility industries, regulation has often been sought because of the inconvenience of competition. The history of regulation is often written in terms of the desire to prohibit "excessive" duplication of utility distribution systems and the desire to prohibit the capture of windfall gains by utility companies. Neither of these aspects of the utility business is necessarily related to scale economies. Let us consider first the problem of excessive duplication of facilities.

**Duplication of Facilities.** Communities and not individuals own or control most of the ground and air rights-of-way used by public utility distribution systems. The problem of excessive duplication of distribution systems is attributable to the failure of communities to set a proper price on the use of these scarce resources. The right to use publicly owned thoroughfares is the right to use a scarce resource. The absence of a price for the use of these resources, a price high enough to reflect the opportunity costs of such alternative uses as the servicing of uninterrupted traffic and unmarred views, will lead to their overutilization. The setting of an appropriate fee for the use of these resources would reduce the degree of duplication to optimal levels.

Consider that portion of the ground controlled by an individual under which a utility's distribution system runs. Confront that individual with the option of service at a lower price from a company that is a rival to the present seller. The individual will take into consideration the cost to him of running a trench through his garden and the benefit to him of receiving the service at lower cost. There is no need for excessive duplication. Indeed, there is no need for any duplication of facilities if he selects the new service, provided that one of two conditions holds. If the individual owns that part of the distribution system running under his ground he could tie it in to whatever trunk line serves him best; alternatively, once the new company wins his patronage, a rational solution to the use of that part of the distribution system would be for the utility company owning it to sell it to the utility company now serving the buyer.

There may be good reasons for using community property rather than private property to house the main trunk lines of some utility distribution systems. The placement of such systems under or over streets, alleyways and sidewalks, resources already publicly owned (a fact taken as datum here), may be less costly than routing them through private property. The failure of communities to charge fees for the use of public property, fees that tend to prevent excessive use of this property, can be explained in three ways:

1. There was a failure to understand the prerequisites for efficient resource use. Some public officer must be given the incentives to act as a rational conservator of resources when these resources are scarce.
2. The disruption of thoroughfares was not, in fact, costly enough to bother about.
3. The setting of fees to curtail excessive use of thoroughfares by utility companies was too costly to be practical.

The first two explanations, if true, give no support to an argument for regulating utility companies. The third explanation may give support to some sort of regulation, for it asserts that the economic effects that are produced by the placing of distribution systems are such that it is too costly to economize through the use of a price system. The costs of taking account of these effects through some regulatory process must be compared with the benefits of realigning resource use, and if the benefits are worth the costs some regulation may be desirable. Note clearly: scale economies in serving a market are not at issue. To see this, imagine that electrical distribution systems are thin lines of a special conducting paint. The placing of such systems causes no difficulties. They are sprayed over either public or private property. Nonetheless, suppose that the use of each system is subject to scale economies. Clearly, the desire to regulate cannot now be justified by such problems as traffic disruption, even though scale economies are present. "Excess" duplication is a problem of externalities and not of scale economies.

Let us suppose that it is desirable to employ some sort of regulation because it is too costly to use the price system to take account of the disruptive effects of placing distribution systems. Regulation comes in all sizes and shapes, and it is by no means clear what type of regulation would be most desirable.

A franchise system that allows only a limited number of utility companies to serve a market area was employed frequently. A franchise system that awarded the franchise to that company which seemed to offer the best price-quality package would be one that allowed market competition between bidding rivals to determine that package. The restraint of the market would be substituted for that of the regulatory commission.

An alternative arrangement would be public ownership of the distribution system. This would involve the collection of competing bids for installing the distribution system. The system could then be installed by the bidder offering to do the specified job at the lowest price. This is the same process used by communities to build highways, and it employs rival bidding and not commissions to determine that price. The community could then allow its distribution system to be used by that utility company offering to provide specified utility services at lowest cost to residents. Again the market is substituted for the regulatory commission. Public ownership of streets may make public ownership of distribution systems seem desirable, but this does not mean that the use of regulatory commissions is desirable.

**The Problem of Windfalls.** We must now consider a last difficulty that has sometimes been marshalled to support the regulation of utilities. This argument is based on the fact that events in life are uncertain. The application of this observation to the utility business goes like this. After a buyer enters into an agreement with a utility company for supplying utility service, there may be changes in technology and prices that make the agreed upon price obsolete. In such cases, it is asserted, the price should be changed to reflect the current cost of providing utility services. The regulation by commission of prices on the basis of current costs is needed in the utilities industries because of the durability of original investments in plant and distribution systems. This durability prohibits the use of recontracting in the market place as a method for bringing about appropriate changes in price.

Problems of uncertainty create a potential for positive or negative windfalls. If market negotiations have misjudged the development of a better technology and if there is some cost to reawarding contracts to other producers once they are agreed upon, then an unexpected improvement in the technology used by those who are awarded the contracts may generate a price that is higher than per-unit cost, but higher by an amount no greater than the cost of reawarding contracts. In such cases, the firms now holding the contracts may collect a positive windfall for a short-run period. Or, if input prices increase by more than is expected, these same firms may suffer from a negative windfall. But the same thing is true of all markets. If a customer buys eggs today for consumption tomorrow, he will enjoy a positive windfall if the price of eggs is higher tomorrow and a negative windfall if the price is lower. The difference in the two cases is that, where long-term contracts are desirable, the windfalls may continue for longer periods. In such cases it may be desirable to employ a cost-plus regulatory scheme or to enter a clause that reserves the right, for some fee, to renegotiate the contract.

The problem faced here is what is the best way to cope with uncertainty. Long-term contracts for the supply of commodities are concluded satisfactorily in the market place without the aid of regulation. These contracts may be between retailers and appliance producers, or between the air lines and aircraft companies, all of whom may use durable production facilities. The rental of office space for ninety-nine years is fraught with uncertainty. I presume that the parties to a contract concluded resolves these issues in a way that is satisfactory to both parties. Penalties for reopening negotiations at a later date can be included in the contract. I presume that buyers and sellers who agree to contract with each other have handled the problem of uncertainty in a mutually satisfactory way. The correct way to view the problem is one of selecting the best type of contract. A producer may say, "if you agree to buy from me for twenty-five years, I can use facilities that are expected to produce the service at lower costs; if you contract five years, I will not invest much in tooling-up, and, hence, I will need a higher price to cover higher per-unit costs; of course, the longer-run contract allows more time for the unexpected, so let us include an escape clause of some kind." The buyer and seller must then agree on a suitable contract; durability of equipment and longer-term commitments can be sacrificed at the cost of higher per-unit costs, but there is no reason to expect that the concluded contract will be biased as to outcome or nonoptimal in other respects.

Cost-plus rate regulation is one way of coping with these problems, but it has great uncertainties of its own. Will the commission be effective? Does a well defined cost-plus arrangement create an inappropriate system of incentives to guide the firm in its investment and operating policies? Do the continual uncertainties associated with the meaning of cost-plus lead to otherwise avoidable difficulties in formulating investment plans? Rate regulation by commissions rather than by market rivalry may be more appropriate for utility industries than for other industries, but the truth of this assertion cannot be established deductively from existing economic theory. We do not know whether regulation handles the uncertainty-rent problem better or worse than the market.

The problem of coping with windfalls must be distinguished from the problem of forecastable rents. Suppose that it is known that buyers will incur considerable recontracting cost if they decide to change sellers after they are part way through an awarded contract. It would appear that the seller who wins the initial contract will be able to collect a rent as large as this recontracting cost. But this is not true if this recontracting cost is forecastable, that is, if it is not a windfall. The bidding for the initial contract will take account of the forecastable rent, so that if the bidding is competitive the rent will be forfeited by the lower bid prices to which it gives rise.

To what degree should legislation and regulation replace the market in the utilities or in other industries and what forms should such legislation take?

It is not the objective of this paper to provide answers to such questions. My purpose has been to question the conventional economic arguments for the existing legislation and regulation. An expanded role for government can be defended on the empirical grounds of a documented general superiority of public administration in these industries or by a philosophical preference for mild socialism. But I do not see how a defense can be based on the formal arguments considered here; these arguments do not allow us to deduce from their assumptions either the monopoly problem or the administrative superiority of regulation.

In the case of utility industries, resorting to the rivalry of the market place would relieve companies of the discomforts of commission regulation. But it would also relieve them of the comfort of legally protected market areas. It is my belief that the rivalry of the open market place disciplines more effectively than do the regulatory processes of the commission. If the managements of utility companies doubt this belief, I suggest that they re-examine the history of their industry to discover just who it was that provided most of the force behind the regulatory movement.

**NOTES TO CHAPTER EIGHT**

1. Antitrust legislation and judicial decision, to the extent that they have been motivated by a concern for bigness and concentration, *per se*, have also benefitted from the asserted relationship between monopoly power and industry structure.

2. Cf., George J. Stigler and Claire Friedland, "What Can Regulators Regulate? The Case of Electricity," *Journal of Law and Economics*, 1962, 5, 1; H. Averch and L. Johnson, "Behavior of the Firm under Regulatory Constraint," *American Economic Review*, December 1962, 52, 1053; Armen Alchian and Reuben Kessel, "Competition, Monopoly, and the Pursuit of Pecuniary Gain," *Aspects of Labor Economics*, 1962, 157.

3. Thus, Milton Friedman, while stating his preference for private monopoly over public monopoly or public regulation, writes, "However, monopoly may also arise because it is technically efficient to have a single producer or enterprise . . . When technical conditions make a monopoly the natural outcome of competitive market forces, there are only three alternatives that seem available: private monopoly, public monopoly, or public regulation." *Capitalism and Freedom*, 1962, 28.

4. Paul A. Samuelson, *Economics*, 6th ed., New York, 1964, 461.

5. Armen Alchian and William R. Allen, *University Economics*, Belmont, California, 1964, 412.

6. I shall not consider in this paper the problem of marginal cost pricing and the various devices, such as multi-part tariffs, that can be used to approximate marginal cost pricing.

7. The competitive concept employed here is not new to economics although it has long been neglected. An early statement of the concept, which

was known as "competition for the field" in distinction to "competition within the field" is given by Edwin Chadwick, "Results of Different Principles of Legislation and Administration in Europe; of Competition for the Field, as compared with the Competition within the Field of Service," *Journal of the Royal Statistical Society*, 1859, 22, 381.

8. Burton N. Behling, *Competition and Monopoly in Public Utility Industries*, 1938, 19-20.

9. However, see George J. Stigler, "A Theory of Oligopoly," *Journal of Political Economy*, February 1964, 72, 44.

# Index

All Channel Receiver Act, p. 80, 85
AMTRAK, p. 21
American Delivery Systems, p. 59
American Management Association, p. 86
American Political Science Association, p. 29
AT&T, p. 43, 44, 71, 73, 74, 93
Anti-Trust, p. 80
Averch-Johnson, pp. 8, 10, 67-77, 100, 101
Averch-Johnson Jubilee, p. 2

Bailey, Elizabeth E., pp. 68, 75, 100
Bain, Joe, p. 10
Bank Holding Company Act, p. 13
Barnett, Harold J., pp. 3, 76, 80-82, 84, 89
Baumol, William, p. 68, 93
Bazelon, David, p. 27
Behling, Burton N., p. 128
Bell Laboratories, pp. 43, 93
Bell Telephone, pp. 40, 43, 45, 59, 72, 93, 119, 121-123
Bernstein, Niel, p. 3
Bonbright, p. 29

CATV, pp. 45, 79-89
Cable Communications, p. 86
Capron, Kahn, Phillips, p. 10
Caterfone decision, pp. 44-46, 59
Chamberlin, Edward, p. 11
Clark, J.B., p. 10
Coase, R.H., p. 125
Coleman, Roger, p. 75
Communications, pp. 43-46
Communications Satellite Corp. (Comsat), pp. 71-73

Competition, inter-area, p. 14
Consolidated Edison, pp. 36, 39
Countermiler, p. 20
Cove Point Project, p. 59
Cox, Kenneth, p. 86

Dordick, H., p. 89
Datran, p. 76
Densetz, Harold, p. 3
Dewey, Donald J., pp. 2, 71, 76
Domestic Satellite Decision, p. 44

E.I.A., p. 89
ETV, pp. 87, 88
Emery, E.D., p. 70
Entry, pp. 5, 11
Executive Branch, p. 56
Expectations, p. 34

FCC, pp. 31, 43-46, 54, 56, 60, 61, 71, 72, 74, 76, 79, 80, 82-88
FDC, p. 45
FDIC, p. 16
FHA, p. 16, 21
Faulhaber, R., p. 93
Federal Energy Commission, p. 49
Federal Power Commission, pp. 31, 43, 46-50
Francis, F.E., p. 48

GPO, p. 83
Gabriel, R.P., p. 20
General Telephone & Electronics, p. 76
Gies, Thomas, pp. 115, 116
Goldmark, Peter, p. 89
Gray, Horace, pp. 1, 3
Greenberg, pp. 80-82, 89

*137*

## 138 Index

Growth, stages of p. 6 et seq.
"gypsy" cabs, pp. 31, 32

Hawaiian Telephone, p. 71
Hope Natural Gas, p. 114
Hughes, p. 48
Hughes, William, p. 70, 76
Hyde, Rosel, p. 86

ICC, pp. 10, 30
Inter-area competition, p. 14

Johnson, Leland L., p. 2
Johnson, Nicholas, p. 86

Kahn, Alfred, p. 29
Kappel Commission, p. 50
Klevorick, Alvin, p. 68
Knight, Frank, pp. 27-29, 36, 38, 39, 71
Kolko, Gabriel, p. 37
Kuhn-Tucker, p. 101

LNG, p. 59
LRIC, pp. 45, 52, 59
Lep, Rex, p. 86

MCI decision, pp. 44, 45, 59, 76
MacAvoy, Paul, pp. 29, 37, 93
Mergers, p. 15
Meyer, B.H., pp. 1, 59
Michigan Bell, pp. 119-122
Microware Communications, Inc., p. 44

Nassikas, Chairman, p. 47
National Cable Television Association (NCTA), p. 88
National Gas Survey, p. 49
National Power Survey, p. 70
National Service Index, p. 53
Natural Gas Shortage, pp. 46-50
Nelson, James R., p. 14
New England Bell, pp. 119, 120, 122, 123
New York Post, p. 31
New York Times, p. 32

Office of Telecommunications Policy, p. 56, 57, 72

PUC, p. 89
Peck, M.J., p. 1
Peltzman, p. 108
Penn Central Railroad, p. 36
Phillips, Charles, p. 29
Pooling, p. 15
Post Office Department, pp. 50, 53
Postal Rate Commission, pp. 43, 50, 52, 54

Postal Rates, pp. 50-54
Profit Maximization, pp. 95, 108
Public Enterprise, pp. 6, 15
public firm competitor, p. 20
Public Service Commission, p. 36
Public Utility Act, p. 13

regulated firm, p. 99
Regulation, multiple, p. 88
Regulatory lag, p. 77
Rocardian rents, p. 81
Rostow, Eugene, p. 86

SRIC, p. 52
Samuelson, p. 126
Schwartz, David S., p. 41
Seagle, William, p. 27, 125
Sharfman, Leo, pp. 10, 29
Shepherd, William G., pp. 70, 115
Shortage, natural gas, p. 46
Simons, Henry, pp. 1, 3, 29
Sloan Commission, pp. 80, 86, 89
Smyth vs. Ames, p. 113
Steiner, p. 95
Stenason, J., p. 1
Stigler, George, pp. 29, 37, 125

TV, pp. 80-89
TVA, pp. 18, 21
Takayama, Akira, p. 68
Tariffs, pp. 44, 103-106
Taxicabs, pp. 30-33
Telpak terriff, p. 44
Theory, developments in, p. 67
Trebing, Harry M., pp. 2, 43

UHF, pp. 80, 84-87
U.S. Department of Agriculture, p. 129
U.S. Postal Service, pp. 50-53
United Parcel Service, pp. 51, 59
Utility Advisory Boards, p. 8
Utility Life Cycle, p. 7
Utility sectors, pp. 6-8

VHF, pp. 80, 87

WHF, p. 80
Wein, Harold, pp. 70, 74
Weiss, Leonard, p. 14
Welfare Maximization, pp. 94-95, 98, 108
Western Electric, p. 43
Western Union, p. 74
Westfield, Fred, p. 68
White, pp. 89, 93

Zajac, E.E., pp. 67, 93
Zwick, C., p. 1

## About the Authors

**William G. Shepherd** is Professor of Economics at the University of Michigan. He has studied regulatory issues extensively, on both a Scholarly and practical basis. His books include *Utility Regulation,* 1966 (co-edited with Thomas G. Gies), *Economic Performance Under Public Enterprise,* 1965, *Market Power and Economic Welfare,* 1970, and *Optimal Industrial Policies: Method and Design in Treating Market Power,* in process. In 1967-8 he was the chief economic adviser at the Antitrust Division, Department of Justice. He is a consultant to numerous private and public groups.

**Thomas G. Gies** is Professor of Finance at the Graduate School of Business Administration, University of Michigan. He has published widely on the economics of financial markets, including their relation to utility financing. He also acts as consultant to a variety of enterprises and public agencies.